Men of the 11th Infantry Regiment move through on a road near Winterburg, Germany 19 March 1945. (National Archives US Army Photo)

FIFTH INFANTRY DIVISION

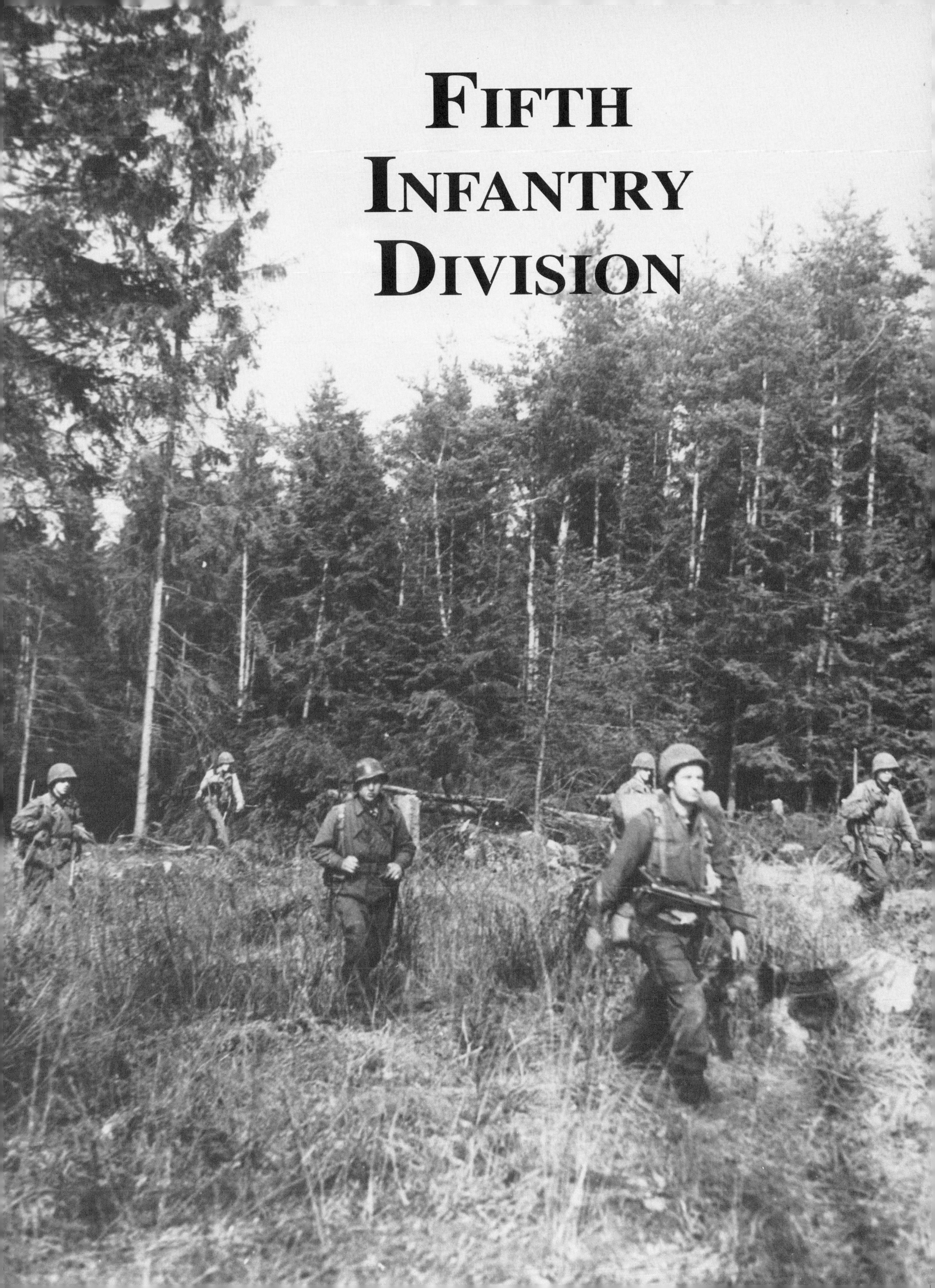

Turner Publishing Company
Publishers of Military History
P.O. Box 3101
Paducah, Kentucky 42002-3101

Co-produced by Mark A. Thompson,
Independent Publishing Consultant
for Turner Publishing Company

Author: David Polk
Book Design: Elizabeth Dennis

Library of Congress Catalog
Card No. : 93-60212

ISBN: 1-56311-060-1

Printed in the United States of America

Limited Edition

Title Page Photo: *Men of the 11th Regiment march across rough ground en route to Winterbach, Germany to clean out German soldiers cut off from their units in retreat 18 March 1945. (National Archives US Army Photo)*

Men of the 10th Infantry Regiment seek refuge behind the stone masonry of a fence from the 20mm gun fire of the unseen Germans 19 February 1945. (National Archives US Army Photo)

"C" Company Mortar Platoon pulls last minute equipment check before returning to Quang Tri Combat Base from a two-day stand down 30 October 1970. (National Archives US Army Photo)

CONTENTS

ACKNOWLEDGMENTS

It is with great pleasure that we introduce this volume on the Fifth Infantry Division, in commemoration of all who served in the Red Diamond Division. The history chronicles the division from activation, through World War I, World War II, Vietnam, Panama, and ending with inactivation on November 24, 1992. For 75 years the Fifth Infantry Division with pride and indomitable spirit proved that their slogan "We Will" was accurate and to the point.

A special heartfelt thanks goes to Joseph G. Rahie. As a great source of information, he contributed many photographs that helped illustrate the complete story of the Fifth Division, and he worked with the publisher to maintain accuracy throughout this publication.

We especially want to thank the many individuals who were responsible for making this book possible, particularly the men who took the time to submit photographs and historical material.

We owe our deepest gratitude to all the personnel of the Fifth Infantry Division for fighting the wars that could have changed our way of life permanently.

Turner Publishing Company leads the way in military association history book publishing, and we hope that the Society of the Fifth Infantry Division enjoys our newest title that chronicles the history of a most courageous division.

Dave Turner, *President* **Mark A. Thompson**, *Associate Publisher*

Past National Presidents

Maj. Gen. Hanson E. Ely	1919-1922
Col. Philip J. McCook	1922-1923
Maj. Gen. Hanson E. Ely	1924-1925
Dr. E. C. Morton	1925-1928
Maj. Gen. Paul B. Malone	1929-1930
Capt.Peter Murphy	1930
Maj. Walter E. Aebischer	1930-1932
Capt. Peter P. Zion	1932-1934
W. Walter Healy	1934-1935
Lloyd A. Rader	1935-1937
Col. Henry Clay Bate	1937-1938
William Barton Bruce, Sr.	1938-1939
Emil Everts	1939-1941
A. Lincoln Bradbury	1941-1945
William Gibbs	1945-1946
John W. Fonner	1946-1948
William L. McGrory	1948-1949
Kenyon Stevenson	1949-1950
Charles A. O'Connell, Jr.	1950-1951
John H. Pflaum	1951-1953
Frederick F. Specht	1953-1954
John H. Baskin	1954-1955
Walter R. Stout	1955-1957
Frank H. Deane	1957-1958
Edward Pivovar	1958-1959
T. Earl McNaney	1959-1960
Russell S. Fisher	1960-1962
Gordon S. Henry	1962-1963
John J. Madison	1963-1965
Herbert K. Webb	1965-1966
Charles P. DeRose	1966-1967
Victor Dunneback	1967-1968
Winston Roche	1968-1969
Ervin J. Kotowski	1969-1970
Herbert Ginsburgh	1970-1971
Aubrey Prewitt	1971-1972
Michael S. O'Donnell	1972-1973
Virgil Scheibel	1973-1974
Frank Kolimaga	1974-1975
Ken Anderson	1975-1976
Howard Singer	1976-1977
Robert Young	1977-1978
Stanley Piotrowski	1978-1979
George W. Bachman	1979-1980
Harry Arquette	1980-1981
William Stanfield	1981-1982
Guido Bernasconi	1982-1983
Msgr. Harold Prudell	1983-1984
Chester Ball	1984-1985
William Colon	1985-1986
Robert Graves	1986-1987
Herman Schell	1987-1988
William Stanfield	1988-1989
John Goodman	1989-1990
William Upham	1990-1991
Bradley Brewer	1991-1992
Harry Arquette	1992-1993

National Officers 1993–1994

President – Robert Rochon
First Vice President – Charles I. Coco
Second Vice President – Hon. Michael Giannini
Secretary – Fred Body
Treasurer – William Colon
Historian – Joseph Rahie
Chaplain – Rev. Roy Doll
Judge Advocate – Frank Fantanza
Editor – Chester Ball

Fifth Division Society

The Fifth Infantry Division Society is 75 years old on June 30, 1994. According to Division historian Joseph G. Rahie, "*the original constitution was adopted, to be effective June 30, 1919,by unanimous vote by the delegates of the Society assembled for the initial meeting of the 'Society of the Fifth Division, US Army, Veterans of the World War,' held at Headquarters of the Fifth Division, USA, Esch-sur-Alzette, Grand Duchy of Luxembourg, on the 11th and 13th of June, 1919. Acting as temporary chairman was Lt.Col. Roger H. Williams, Assistant Chief of Staff, G-2, Fifth Division.*"

Mr. Rahie goes on: "*This was the beginning. The organization has continued without interruption to the present day, making it the oldest divisional society, in years of service, in existence. Although the Society has enjoyed a long and distinquished life, the road was not always smooth and trouble-free, and its very existence was at times in peril.*"

"*During the post-World War I period, from 1922 to 1927, it appeared the Society would go under, as most of the other divisional societies had done. However, a dedicated few stepped in to take the reins and led the organization through trying times. All through our history we have been fortunate to have members who, through their great loyalty to the Society, contributed their time and personal funds to the continuation of the Society of the Fifth as we know it today. Thus, the Society continued, although having been at a dangerously low ebb at times, from its beginning in Luxembourg in 1919 to the present time, a span of 75 years.*"

The Society of the Fifth Division, USA, exists "*to perpetuate and memorialize the valiant acts and patriotic deeds of the Fifth Division; to electrify and unify that invisible current of fellowship and comradeship moulded in the throes of war, and to promote the interests and welfare of the members of the Society; to uphold the Constitution of the USA and to perpertuate and foster true Americanism; to assist worthy comrades and to preserve the historical records of the Fifth Division in the World Wars.*"

"*We have come a long way,*" wrote Mr. Rahie in the Society's newsletter **The Red Diamond**. "*The length of service and the robust condition of the Society today can be attributed to the dedication, comradeship, and friendship the founders set out to instill in the organization at its inception.*"

"Happy Birthday, Red Diamond!"

Jos. G. Rahie
National Historian

FIFTH INFANTRY DIVISION

Members of Baker Co. with tank support move up through the woods outside the town of Neuheim, en route to Schwanheim, Germany in February of 1945. (National Archives US Army Photo)

THE BEGINNING OF THE FIFTH INFANTRY DIVISION

Earliest History Of The Fifth

The Fifth Infantry Division, the famed Red Diamond Division, was a spearhead for General George S. Patton's Third Army in a number of the most important battles of World War II. If that were the sum of its record, that alone would make a heavyweight place for it in American military history. But it had already distinguished itself 26 years earlier in World War I against the same German enemy. During the Korean War, the Fifth was a major force in training combat replacements troops. Then the 1st Brigade, Fifth Division (Mechanized) served in Vietnam from 1968 to 1971.

We can safely say, therefore, that the Fifth Infantry Division has been in the foreground of our nation's fighting ranks throughout this century. This accounts for the enormous pride of its fighting men and their leaders in every chapter of its history—and the esprit de corps one encounters even in its oldest veterans.

That is still not the sum of it, however. As a whole unit of the size we know it today, the Fifth Infantry Division made its first attack in France on August 17, 1918, but some of its elements can trace their lineage back to the 19th and even the 18th century. Organic units of the Fifth fought in the Indian Wars of the late 1700s under Gen. Anthony Wayne, a Revolutionary War veteran. Furthermore, what were to become Fifth Infantry Division units fought at the Battle of New Orleans in the War of 1812, the Civil War, and the Spanish American War of 1898.

A good example of an historic member of the Fifth as we know it today is the venerable 2nd Infantry Regiment—organized under a bill signed by President George Washington. Its first Indian campaign against the Miami Indians under Chief Little Turtle led to a defeat on November 4, 1791, and one might use as the date of the first bloodshed of a unit that was to father the Fifth. (Thus, the history of the Fifth Division might be said to date back at least 203 years). The 2nd Regiment was to even the score of that first defeat when—under Gen. Wayne—it won a major victory against the Native Americans on August 20, 1794, on the bank of the Maumee River near Fort Deposit—the present town of Waterville, Ohio.

Succeeding years saw the 2nd moving here and there mopping up after skirmishes with various tribes and settling briefly at various posts throughout the Midwest. And if space allowed we might follow it into the War of 1812, the Mexican War, and so on into our present century.

Another good example of these earliest units would be the 10th Infantry Regiment formed even before our Civil War, and it too distinguished itself in the Indian Wars. The 10th dates it inception to March 3, 1855 at which time the Sioux tribesmen were fighting desperately against the encroaching settlers in the middle West.

Col. E.B. Alexander addressed the newly fledged 10th as he presented them with their national and regimental colors: "*In your hands and your courage and fidelity are now entrusted the honor of your country and the reputation of your corps. In time of peace so conduct yourselves that neither (of your colors) shall be sullied. In time of war, in the presence of the enemy, remember that these colors which I present to you now are far more precious than life itself.*"

Broken into detachments for frontier fighting, the men of the 10th rode out from Fort Snelling, Minnesota, to meet the Native Americans—Sioux, Comanche, Yankton, Apache, and Navajo. The 10th fought from the Platte River to the Great Horn, from the Red to the Badlands, and by 1862 had done its part in subduing the Indian force in this area of the continent and making a way for our westward expansion. The Civil War was raging then, of course, and the 10th moved on to that crimson field.

And last but not least—in our search for the roots of the Fifth, there is the Civil War origins of the 11th Infantry Regiment. President Abraham Lincoln signed the bill May 4, 1861 authorizing this regiment's organization as 2nd Battalion, 15th Infantry. Although as far back as 1798 there were regiments which bore this number, the 11th which so distinguished itself in the two World Wars emerged from the old 24th and 29th Infantry Regiments at the end of the Civil War.

During the Civil War, the 11th's men were a part of the Army of the Ohio and then the Army of the Cumberland. They fought in battles in Tennessee, Kentucky, and Georgia—including such important places as Shiloh, the Kentucky Campaign, Chickamauga, the March through Georgia, and the Battle of Atlanta.

After the war, the 11th was also active in the Indian Campaigns along our expanding western frontiers until near 1900. This was interrupted only by a period of garrison life from 1887 to 1891. Then during our war with Spain in 1898, it took part in the conquest and pacification of Puerto Rico, and shortly thereafter was fighting in the Philippines.

WORLD WAR I

The Fifth As We Know It Begins

And thus, the 5th Infantry Division can look back across time to a past and a tradition with much pride. But the fully assembled Fifth Division made its debut in World War I after it was activated at Camp Logan, Texas, on December 1st, 1917.

The famous Red Diamond was chosen for the division insignia at about this time. A brief recap of its origin goes like this: Major Charles A. Meals of the Quartermaster Corps was informed that a distinctive emblem was in order for this new division, and his suggestion was "*the ace of diamonds minus the ace.*" The idea was approved by General McMahon and officially adopted in General Order No. 2, January 18, 1918. The order stated: "*The division insignia will be a Red Diamond with a vertical diagonal of six inches and a horizontal diagonal of four inches in the center of which will be a two inch figure '5' in white.*" After reaching France, the figure '5' was dropped from the diamond. In succeeding years, the Red Diamond was reduced to its present size.

Major General Charles H. Muir was the Division's first commander. Assigned to his command at this time were some of the most historically outstanding regiments in our early history. At its inception, there was the 9th Infantry Brigade composed of the new 60th and 61st Infantry Regiments and the 14th Machine Gun Battalion; the 10th Infantry Brigade composed of the 6th and 11th Infantry Regiments and the 15th Machine Gun Battalion; finally, the 5th Field Artillery Brigade composed of the 19th, 20th, and 21st Field Artillery Regiments and the 5th Trench Mortar Battalion. Major General John E. McMahon succeeded Gen. Muir in this training phase of the new division.

February 24, 1918, less than three months after activation, the Division's sailing orders were received, and therefore it was never to come together as a whole at Camp Logan as planned. Why? The Red Diamond men were badly needed in Europe—there was a long bloody stalemate waiting to be resolved, and the Division slogan was to be "We will."

Billeting and training units were sent to France first to hastily prepare a place for the flood of green troops who would soon arrive. They would ship out piecemeal in the next few weeks and find their way to areas in the British Isles and France. Division Headquarters was established May 1, 1918, at Le Havre, France, a northern port city close to Paris. The 7th Engineers and the 7th Engineer train were among the first to arrive and begin operations for obvious reasons. As units began to arrive, they immediately continued their combat training in earnest. The doughboys were close enough now to catch wind of the killing fields known as "No Man's Land."

Background To WW I

But let us back off briefly here, and sketch in the background prior to this arrival of the 5th Infantry Division for the first time on foreign shores. At this point, the war had dragged on since August, 1914, a war most on either side thought would not last long. A German General Staff Officer had said early on it would take no more than four months to cut down "*those dreaming sheep*" by which he meant the allied French, British, and Russians. But the Central Powers—primarily Germany and Austro/Hungarian empire—would, of course, not have it that easy.

The United States, which had declared neutrality when war first broke out in 1914, had done it best to keep its distance from the unprecedented slaughter. President Woodrow Wilson had steered as straight a course between the belligerents as one could hope for, but the odds were always against him. Although there were many German immigrants and U.S. citizens of German and Austrian descent, Britain was our long-time trading partner with whom we shared a common history, and so from the start we leaned in that direction.

What's more, in the media of the time—primarily newspapers and magazines, the Allies were winning the propaganda war. The Germans alienated many Americans by violating Belgian neutrality right off the bat when they bombed Antwerp. It was also hard not to notice the Prussian arrogance in much the German war machine accomplished. The intimidating tales of the "Hun's atrocities" abounded.

Furthermore, evidence was discovered which showed the Germans had shipped arms to Mexico even before 1914—weapons to be used against the United States; the Germans had even offered to return to Mexico—after the Central Powers victory—"the lost territory of Texas, New Mexico, and Arizona."

On May 7, 1915, Americans died when the Germans sank the famous Lusitania, yet another obvious sign that they did not think the US a serious threat. A major U-boat offensive was launched February 1, 1917, against the shipping of all nations, and many more Americans were to die at sea. Clearly, the German high command was certain it would take the US too long to mobilize should we ever decide to act.

Historians today agree that at this point the only way we could have continued our neutral stand was to break off all our ties to Europe, but that was by then simply impossible. As historian John H. Moore put it, "*For better or worse, the United States was an integral part of the Atlantic world, and thus had a share in its promises, problems, and profits, whatever the cost might be.*" And thus, at one stroke our long isolationist position ended, and our European commitment was born—a deep and serious involvement which has lasted even down to the time of this writing, 1994.

So, soon after the new U-boat offensive, President Wilson broke off diplomatic relations with the Germans, and then April 6, 1917, he asked Congress for a declaration of war. In his famous speech, he called for "*force, force to the utmost, force without stint or limit.*"

From that date, we were part of a war that had no precedent in it scope, its technology, and it devastation. Only World War II compares or goes beyond it. When the war began in 1914, six to seven million men took up arms against each other. The President stated in May, 1917, this was a war of nations as much as armies, and those nations numbered 23 before it was over. Historian Hanson Baldwin put it this way: "*never before 1914-18 had a war absorbed so much of the total resources of so many combatants and covered so large a part of the earth. Never had so many nations been involved. Never had the slaughter been so comprehensive and indiscriminate. The submarine, the plane, the machine gun, the tank, and poison gas wrote new and foreboding chapters in the history of war.*"

In the light of this hellish prospect, one cannot fault President Wilson for holding back the course of history so long—he had seen the casualty reports from the war's beginning in 1914. The Allies had suffered somewhere near a million and a half casualties in the first five months alone. During 1916 at Verdun alone there were several million casualties, and a million more in Flanders, and yet another million on the eastern front. The figures are still staggering to review—and always will be, one hopes. Did our country want to rush our young men into this ungodly blood-letting?

Yes, that is what the doughboys of the Fifth Infantry Division had waiting for them. Willing, optimistic, untrained and inexperienced, they were to be dropped into the middle of this holocaust. They were expected to tip the balance in this four year stalemate between the Allies and the Central Powers, and they did. Two million American soldiers were to arrive in Europe before the war was over, and the Fifth was among those who fought the hardest.

The Fifth's Fiery Baptism

The year 1917 had gone poorly for the Allies. The French took a long while to recover from the monumental Allied failure in May of 1917 which was blamed on the French General Robert Nivelle who led the offensive. It had ended with 120,000 French soldiers needlessly slaughtered. Mutiny spread through the French ranks. The Russian Revolution has allowed the Germans to free up soldiers on the Eastern Front. The Italians, our Allies also, were doing poorly against the Austro-Hungarians.

Yes, 1917 had left the Allies severely strapped, and the doughboys were sorely needed as quickly as possible. By New Year's day, they were pouring into France but there was still only 100,000 in country. When the units of the Fifth Infantry Division were first arriving early in France in 1918, the Germans were beginning their big offensive push to win at any cost. It began in March when they begin driving down the Somme Valley. This was intimidating to the say the least for the young Red Diamond men.

Gen. Mark Clark recalled sailing for Europe on the ship Leviathan, "*God, I think the whole 5th Division was on that one ship! And she was a fast one; didn't even need a convoy, she could outrun any submarine. I can't remember how long the trip took, but it seemed that we were in Brest, France in no time at all!*"

By May 1, 1918, all the Fifth Infantry Division units were in France and assembled for the first time. Intensive training was of course the next step for these green troops. These "raw recruits" were only slightly leavened by some seasoned career soldiers. One thing in particular distinguished them from any other American army—the veteran NCOs were given extraordinary respect and authority, and this was enforced even by the officers.

In addition, the battle-weary veterans from the French and British armies proceeded to teach them what they had learned. This included intense sharpshooter exercises with a poor weapon, the Model 1917 rifle, (awkward and crudely tooled), artillery gunning practice, the art of gas warfare, and so on.

General John J. Pershing, the Commander in Chief of the American Expeditionary Forces, made his inspection of the division a scant few weeks later and judged the men ready to move to the front—but is it likely they were so quickly battle-ready?

Be that as it may, on May 31, the Fifth's "Field Order No. 1" was issued—and our Division was on the way to its first combat zone. They were ready to roll; their motto was, of course, "We will" to the call of duty. Their favorite expression was, "Start arguin', bastards."

Brig. Gen. S.L.S. Marshall writes that "*There has never been a prouder, happier, more talkative army under the American flag. Amid snafus, which were frequent, some joker invariably would sound off with that pet AEF phrase: 'She said there'd be days like this.' As they marched over the old Roman roads, they sang the bawdiest songs within memory.*" The General goes on to say that when they fought, they whooped it up as if the battle field were a football stadium. (It can't all have been that cheerful, but this was a young and—compared to our era—a naive generation).

As was customary with new units, to begin with they were put under the command of a veteran Allied force in an out-of-the-way sector of the front—in this case the French Seventh Army in the upper Alsace and Vosges Mountains—where, incidentally, their World War II "descendants" would fight so bravely. Here the men of the Fifth were to learn more about trench warfare in the trenches themselves. Some of the division units were further detached to join the French XXXIII Corps.

At this time, Mark Clark, later to be a General and one of the foremost soldiers of our century, was a brand new captain and commander of K Co., 11th Infantry of the Fifth Division. Back in the states, Lt. Clark—not long out of West Point—had helped form the Fifth at Chickamauga Park with some of his fellow graduates. The Fifth was part of I Corps, he recalls, under the command of Gen. Pershing. Capt. Clark reminisces at length in a book called **Make the Kaiser Dance**, and gives us a good feel for what life was like for the soldier of the Fifth in 1918.

After a train ride across France, Capt. Clark reports, "*finally we're out in the middle of nowhere, and I'm told to take K Co. off the train. Then they gave me a little map and told me to march them to a town named Fresney, down in the Vosges Mountains.*"

Once they arrived, to his amazement, "*This farmer came out to greet us. He must have been the richest man in town because the manure pile in front of his house was the biggest.*" The townspeople were overjoyed to see the Yanks for obvious reasons. There was hardly a French family which had not lost a member in the war, and their hatred of the Central Powers and their desire to rid their land of them was understandably intense. But in addition, they would be paid a franc a day for each soldier they put up in a barn or wherever. And they would also be selling wine to the Americans—and whatever else might be in demand.

After settling in, Capt. Clark took off on a bicycle to try to find his battalion headquarters—he had no idea where the rest of the Division was! Thus, the state of our AEF communications network at this point. Regimental headquarters was about 20 kilometers away it turned out. When asked, he told the old Colonel at HQ that he had ridden a bicycle to get there. "*Of course you did, you damn fool,*" the colonel growled, "*and how do you think it looked to the French to see an American captain riding a woman's bicycle*?" One point to Clark's story is to emphasize how old-fashioned and just plain old many superior officers were. Kidding aside, many of these career officers were simply not prepared for modern warfare.

Capt. Clark then describes the training which followed for the next three weeks which included bayonet drill and 20 mile hikes. "*We couldn't waste a minute, because we knew what was ahead.*" Soon then, word from HQ came down, "*Full marching gear men, it's our turn now.*" He goes on, "*Now for the amazing part. Just before we went into the front lines, I received new orders that Maj. Kingman was sick, and I was to take the battalion into combat. Poor Kingman, he was too old to be there anyway...and here I am, 22 years of age and I have command of a thousand men in combat. The area was called St. Die....*"

St. Die had for a long while—like many sectors along the great western front—been a "static sector." Such was the nature of trench warfare. "*It was called a quiet sector,*" observed Capt. Clark, "*but the Germans had a nasty habit of frequently sending over shells when they knew an American outfit was moving in. This was in the Alace-Lorraine where the Germans had a hundred spies. Hell, they knew the Fifth was going in, and where, before most of us did.*"

Observation Post of the 6th Infantry near Croix de Charemont in St. Die Sector 15 July 1918. (Courtesy of Joseph G. Rahie)

In this area, the Germans had held "No Man's Land" for more than three years. But not long after they arrived, the Red Diamond patrols reversed that situation. They increased their patrol activities and soon enough had control of that turf.

"*I had no sooner disposed of my three companies in the lines, holding the fourth in reserve*," recalls Capt. Clark of that historic day in June, "*when they let us have it. Being young and eager, I felt I should start inspecting the units to make sure no one panicked. That's when I caught it; the divisional history says I was the first man in the Fifth wounded. It was bad. Shrapnel hit my right knee, shoulder, and worst of all, right near the spine. I'll always remember that date, because it was our first day on the lines: June 12, 1918.*"

Removed to a French hospital, Clark was operated on by French surgeons quite effectively. Nevertheless, he was relieved to be transferred to an American hospital in a short while. He praises the American medical corps personnel to the skies, and makes clear how much the nurses did for his health and his morale. And thankfully, he recovered to go on with his distinguished career. (Later, his comments on the Fifth's involvement in the Meuse-Argonne campaign will be reported).

Now, let's have some brief background to this offensive at St. Die which involved the Fifth. August 10, Gen. "Black Jack" Pershing took command of the US First Army. Very quickly then, the plans for the first All-American offensive were drawn up. On August 15, the plan was in Pershing's hands; the French commander Marshall Ferdinand Foch liked it so much he added six French divisions—and our Gen. Pershing would have command of it all.

In general, our highly secret plan was to "*nip off the St. Mihiel salient, straighten out the line, and there halt, regardless of the German reaction and the rich prizes lying beyond*," wrote Gen. S.L.A. Marshall. As part of I Corps, the Fifth Infantry Division was on the far right—near the eastern end—of the offensive (including the 11th Regiment in the Vosges mountain area). This German salient had been intact for four years, and the French had made little effort to change it. The trench lines here averaged about a half mile apart. Up to this point, Marshall reports that although aerial dogfights occurred everyday and there were intermittent gas attacks, sometimes German bands played concerts in the front lines in the evening, and American patrols sneaked closer for a listen; that is how used to the stalemate both sides had become.

Part of the moving into place for this big attack at St. Mihiel occasioned the Fifth Infantry Division's fiery baptism as a whole unit on August 17th. It made "*its first concerted attack up the valley towards St. Die*," according to the Fifth Division historians. He concludes that, in general, "*The attack was successful and resulted in the capture of two strategically important points, Hill 451 and the village of Frapple. But most important of all, it resulted in the first change in the German lines since 1915.*"

The St. Mihiel Offensive

Subsequently on August 20, the Fifth was relieved and moved to the Arches for R & R and further training in preparation for St. Mihiel as the build-up continued. The American Expeditionary Force was nearing a million men now. On August 28, the Fifth began assembling in the Moselle River area. On September 4, the division "*began a gruelling 50 kilometer march through mud and rain to the front*", write Division historians. "*At the front, it was assigned a zone two kilometer's wide, and a tough objective of enemy strongly entrenched in hills in the Meuse Valley.*"

The Fifth was placed between the 2nd and the 90th Infantry Divisions also of I Corps. The stage was set. Sixteen American divisions in all were deployed. From the Moselle River in the east to Haudiomont in the west, from flank to flank 665,000 soldiers were assembled. Moreover, 3,220 artillery pieces were in place. A fleet of 1,500 planes were at ready—primitive and unwieldy, of course; (the Wright brothers had flown at Kitty Hawk scarcely a decade before). In addition, 267 tanks were to be cranked up—the American Tank Corps would man some of these in its first combat role under a little known Col. George S. Patton, Jr. whose association with the Fifth in World War II is historic.

Now, under the Generals Fuchs and Gallwitz, the Germans knew an attack was imminent and that it would probably come across the Woevre Plain, but they did not know that it would come from both sides of the salient until September 9. A hasty change of German plans called for a withdrawal beginning September 10, but it went too slowly. It had hardly begun when the doughboys came out of their trenches with a vengeance.

September 12 at 1:00 a.m., the American artillery bombardment began. It was what they call a "buster," that is, a relentless rain of fire down on the Germans. At 5:00 a.m., the doughboys "went over the top." Here is General Marshall on I Corps and the Red Diamond advance: "*on the southern face of the salient it went as rapidly as tired men can move across badly broken ground.*" There were endless tangles of barbed wire, craters, mud, felled trees, and debris of every sort—a rat's haven.

"*The first waves*," the General goes on, "*overran the enemy front line trenches, capturing Germans in swarms as they emerged hands in the air from their dugouts. Before noontime, the divisions of I Corps captured Fey-de-Haye, Vieville-en-Haye, and Thiaucourt on the Army objective line, after cleaning out a vicious complex of machine gun nests in a gas-filled blind valley called Stumpf Laager.*"

There was also heavy fighting on the salient's other side by IV and V Corps, and by the end of the first day, most of the objectives for the second day had also been reached. Then by the morning of the second day, the St. Mihiel salient had passed into American hands. The first American offensive had yielded 15,000 prisoners and 257 guns, and succeeded in taking back 200 square miles of French territory from the enemy. The men of the Red Diamond had been an important factor in this success.

The I Corps Commander, Major General Hunter Liggett sent this message to the fighting men of the Fifth after their first day on the offensive: "*Congratulate sincerely the 5th Division on its splendid achievement today and express my pride and gratification in having such a splendid unit under my command.*" Five officers and 16 enlisted men of the Fifth were awarded the Distinguished Service Cross.

The Fifth was relieved on September 16th. And in the aftermath, it seemed clear that if the French battle plan had not dictated the Americans stop, they could have easily gone on to a monumental victory. Gen. Pershing in his report stated: "*Without doubt continuation of the advance would carried us well beyond the Hindenburg line and possible into Metz.*"

Like the other divisions on a brief R & R, the Fifth relaxed in a quiet French village, eating all they could of the local cheese, sausage and beer, and watching the local vintners use their feet to squeeze the best from their grapes. Meanwhile, other offensives were being readied in the Ypres-Lys region and on the Somme—and in the Meuse-Argonne area. It was during this respite that Major General Hanson E. Ely succeeded General McMahon as the Fifth Division commander.

The Meuse-Argonne Offensive

As the Fifth rested and received replacements, Capt. Mark Clark and many others under Col. George C. Marshall were working out transportation for moving 820,000 men including the Fifth into place for the Meuse-Argonne offensive. It was scheduled to begin only 12 days after the mop-up at St. Mihiel. Troops moved in trucks at night with their lights out along three main roads mired in mud and pot holes. It was rainy and cold, and mosquitoes are horrible this time of year in this part of France.

In the days shortly before the offensive, the American effort to fool the Germans worked who expected the major attack at Metz. The "no man's land" which the Fifth and, in general, all the divisions of Pershing's First Army faced was described this way by Gen. S.L.A. Marshall: "*the Germans had established four successive defensive belts along the Meuse and almost double that on the Argonne end. Until they played sitting war with the Communist Chinese in Korea, it was the thickest and most elaborated ramified earthworks zone ever assaulted by US troops. Far more wire, steel, and concrete bulwarked the German system.*"

What's more, "*the terrain was so repellent as to suggest that nature had designed it to serve as a barrier.*" This included a hogback with spurs, back switches and saddles, rock-bound citadels, rivers, and between them the Argonne Forest with its tree-covered heights. In short, "*From stage center and both wings, the enemy was looking right down the American throat.*" Pershing had accepted the assignment from Marshall Foch. The Red Diamond men, too, said, "WE will."

September 26, D-Day, the Fifth was ready in place on the far left and its goal—along with the rest of I Corps was to advance along through the Argonne Forest west and north to the Meuse River.

They were, however, held in reserve at first, and they would be sorely needed because in the notorious Argonne Forest, the American advance soon bogged down on the first day. On day two, although it pushed down the valley I Corps was stopped again in the Argonne. Gen. Marshall reports: "*By nightfall, the front was in a state of disorganization.*" Here as elsewhere the Germans were using their superior and well-protected positions to wreak havoc on the doughboys. "*Among the Americans, the confusions that mounted rapidly after the first day turned to stagnation and then to paralysis as September ended.*"

Nevertheless, there was Allied progress on several other fronts, and on October 2 back in Germany Gen. Ludendorff warned the Reichstag that defeat was just around the corner. It was clear by now that the Americans had in fact turned the tide in favor of the exhausted French and British. On October 3, at Ludendorff's bequest, Supreme Commander Paul von Hindenburg urged that a peace offer go out to the Allies. Germany was ripe for mutiny and revolution at home by this point.

Burial of 5th Infantry Division casualties at Orchard Cemetery, south of Nantillois in October of 1918. (Courtesy of Joseph Rahie)

G-2 Office at Bois de Tuilerie 20 October 1918. (Courtesy of Joseph Rahie)

Then when the Allied attack was resumed on October 4, the new German Chancellor Max of Baden sent a cable to President Wilson in Washington proposing an armistice. But no one on the battlefields knew of or was directly affected these things, of course, and, for I Corps, the Argonne was still the stop gap where American blood flowed ceaselessly.

The Fifth was first ordered into the frontlines on October 11 under heavy artillery fire to relieve the 80th Division. Three days later they attacked with brigade abreast—sweeping through the Bois de la Pultiere on October 15. It was hell there in the Argonne. Troops were lost in the ravined, broken land of the forest. Gen. Marshall reports that "*Guns and heavy trucks could not pass through it. Within it, a soldier's horizon is limited to grenade range. Units found their way by guess or dead reckoning.*" But, of course, the Germans knew the area well and "*had every trail covered and every height crowned with a machine gun nest.*"

By October 21, after fierce fighting the Fifth had captured another section of the Argonne called Bois des Rappes. On October 22, they were relieved and sent to Montfaucon for rest and rehabilitation. At this point, they had already suffered 4,449 casualties—779 killed in action, 3108 wounded, and 562 gassed.

The second phase of this campaign started on October 26 for the Red Diamond men. Little did they know when they began this offensive that it would last until the end of the war. Moving over the small hills and through the blood-soaked valleys, they drove the Germans north and by November 3 held positions along the Meuse River. Crossing this river was an absolute necessity strategically, and here are the words of one Division historian on this crucial moment:

The enemy "*had concentrated a tremendous fire power along the river and the Canal de l'Est which ran roughly parallel to the larger stream for some distance. Machine guns, mortars, and one pounders covered virtually every square foot of ground across which the troops would have to advance.*" A great tradition of crossing fiercely contested rivers was about to be born to the Fifth Division.

"Bridge sites were picked by patrols of the 6th and 60th Infantry Regiments, and a footbridge was put across the river on the night of November 2. Under cover of darkness that night, Co. G, 6th Infantry, filtered across the footbridge to reinforce Co. E which had gone over before and was holding a position under the bank of the Canal l'Est. The troops worked down the canal a distance of 600 meters during the day, carrying bridge material, and that night footbridges were built across the canal, but the men who went across encountered heavy fire from the strongly held enemy positions."

"All day November 4, a small force of infantry held the canal bank while the enemy poured out its maximum fire in a futile effort to dislodge them. Just after dusk, companies E and G less two platoons reached the eastern bank, wiped out the machine gun nests and established a bridgehead—gaining the first foothold across the Meuse. The remainder of the 9th Brigade followed and the entire 10th Brigade was across the river and canal and in position for further attack by daylight November 5. A combat wagon of the 11th Infantry was the first American vehicle to cross the Meuse."

"Once the crossing had been forced, the Fifth Division went on to establish bridgeheads for both its neighboring divisions and then continued to push on across the heights from which the enemy had been driven, advancing 18 kilometers of territory before the Armistice on November 11 brought hostilities to a close. For this successful crossing the Fifth paid heavily in blood and limb: 2,122 casualties."

General Pershing himself took special notice of this achievement in a letter to General Ely in April 1919: "*The feat of arms...which marks especially the Fifth Division's ability as a fighting unit was the crossing of the Meuse and the establishment of a bridgehead on the eastern bank. This operation was one of the most brilliant feats in the history of the American Army in France.*"

General Pershing summed up the Meuse-Argonne offensive this way, " Between September *26 and November 11, 22 American and 4 French divisions—on a front extending*

Heavy pontoon bridge at Dun constructed by Co. B & E, 7th Engineers 5 November 1918. (Courtesy of Joseph Rahie)

Remoiville seized by 2nd Battalion, 11th Infantry on 9 November 1918. (Courtesy of Joseph Rahie)

from southeast of Verdun to the Argonne Forest—engaged and decisively defeated 46 different German divisions representing 25% of the enemy's entire divisional strength on the Western Front...." He went on to point out that 1,200,000 men were engaged in the 47 days of fighting—the greatest battle of American history until World War II. And the Fifth Infantry Division was a major factor in that long, decisive battle.

The Fifth Division Artillery moving up a "French 75" by hand. (Courtesy of Joseph Rahie)

A majority of the Fifth's casualties occurred in October when the fighting was the fiercest in and around the Argonne and along the Meuse and beyond. They were particularly hard hit going against the Kriemhilde Stellung. Included in the casualties there was Sam Woodfill of the Fifth Division, a Congressional Medal of Honor winner and a man who Gen. Pershing called the outstanding "old Army" soldier of the war.

Bridge being repaired in Dun by the Fifth. (Courtesy of Joseph Rahie)

Capt. Sam Woodfill's story is worth recounting as an example of the courage of the Fifth Division in general in the Meuse-Argonne. A farmboy from Indian Kentuck Creek in Jefferson County, Indiana, Sam was a crack shot and had been in action as an infantryman in the Philippines. Our American Army was not much more than 100,000 men strong when we entered World War I, and veteran officers were in short supply as we have seen. So Sam was commissioned, then helped form the Fifth—a division that was officially supposed to be composed of regular army personnel but in fact was not.

In the Meuse-Argonne campaign, the German machine gun nests were the nemesis of many a Red Diamond man and knocking them out was to be Capt. Woodfill's specialty. This report is from Woodfill's comrade in arms John Gilbertie.

"*It all started for Sam at 6:00 on October 13 when he moved his men into No Man's Land. The Germans' Maxims were waiting for them. They tore holes in Sam's ranks—Company M, 60th Infantry. He jumped into a shell hole to try to size things up, but chose the wrong hole...it was loaded with lingering mustard gas. Woodfill stayed long enough to locate three groups of Germans. Then he proceeded to work himself into a position where he could bring his Springfield (rifle) into play. Before he was through, Sam had eliminated five*

German gun crews, using his rifle for most of them, but also chipping in with his automatic and even a German pick axe. (He had killed 19 of the enemy). He didn't quit until he collapsed from the gas he had inhaled earlier (and he was wounded in the left leg as well). They moved him back to a hospital near Bordeaux where he almost died of the pneumonia (which often followed exposure to such gas)."

Capt. Sam Woodfill received the Congressional Medal of Honor for his valor in this campaign. As he lay in the hospital, however, nothing could console him when he read the list of men in his company who had been killed. It included a recent Italian emigrant, Johnny Pulcino, a favorite of Woodfill's even though he—a green recruit—had failed to gain much in rifle training. Woodfill had realized "*the advance was going to be rough and had sent Pulcino back of the lines on stretcher detail. Nevertheless, a German shell found Johnny sitting in a dugout. At least ten people told me*," the aging veteran Mr. Gilbertie concluded, "*that there was just no haven in the Meuse-Argonne*."

(Years later, Sam Woodfill's file was dusted off and he was brought back in World War II as a major in charge of one of the largest rifle ranges for training GIs in the country).

It was aggressive action such as Sam Woodfill's which caused one historian to call "*the Red Diamond the emblem of the Meuse Division. It is the diamond that, after slowly grinding the Boche from out of the Bois des Rappes, became the point of the arrow that pierced the Meuse River*." Thus, the 11th Infantry Regiment has chosen the day of November 5—the crossing of the Meuse—as its Organization Day, and adopted the stirring French march "Sombre et Meuse" for its regimental march.

When the armistice came—November 11—Capt. Mark Clark recalled: "*Actually, I was not far from my old outfit, the 11th Infantry, at the time. My, but they'd been shot up there, just dreadful, perfectly dreadful!*" Throughout the war, the Fifth Infantry Division suffered 9,299 casualties. This included 1,362 killed in action, 329 who died of wounds, 6182 wounded in action, 1,110 gassed in action, 256 missing in action, and 60 taken prisoner.

Fifth Division Regiments were east of the River Loison when the Armistice went into effect 11 November 1918. (Courtesy of Joseph Rahie)

Sixth Infantry Regiment was part of the Army of Occupation at Treves in November 1918. (Courtesy of Joseph Rahie)

BETWEEN THE WORLD WARS

The Fifth Between The Wars

After the armistice, the Fifth was ordered to be one of the ten divisions chosen as the army of occupation in the terms of the peace treaty with the Germans. The Fifth Division's base of operations was the tiny Grand Duchy of Luxembourg which was right across the northern French border, not far north of the Meuse River which the Fifth had fought so hard to cross, and bordered on one side by Germany. Coincidentally, the Fifth would be back to defend Luxembourg in World War II which we shall see later.

The Fifth's occupation duties ended July 4, 1919, and it began to ship back out for home. Even as they departed, of course, Corporal Adolf Hitler, an insanely bitter German soldier who had been temporarily blinded in combat had already pledged himself to a life of political revenge—against the German leaders he felt betrayed his army, and, of course, against the Allies who defeated them. Less than 25 years from now, the Fifth—including some men who fought in the battles we have just recounted—would be returning to drive back the legions of this corporal.

Back in the states, the veterans of the Fifth were discharged at Camps Meritt and Mills, and on October 4, 1921, three years after its valorous service in the Meuse-Argonne, the Red Diamond division was deactivated.

The Second Infantry Regiment (which was to become a Fifth Division element) spent World War I in charge of captured German ships in Honolulu Harbor and performed other valuable service in that area. What happened to the Second between the wars was typical of other units as well—it was reduced to one battalion and a regimental headquarters. It was then ordered to Fort Sheridan, Illinois where it was a mainstay in a troop training center. Various redesignations and changes of stations took place in the next 18 years. Eventually, the regiment was assigned to newly reactivated Fifth Infantry Division on October 16, 1939 at which time the whole Army was beginning to gear up for possible entry into World War II. The units of the Fifth were being assembled at Fort McClellan, Alabama under the command of Gen. Thomas B. Hodges. And it is here we pick up the narrative of the Red Diamond Division again.

The 11th Infantry Regiment enjoyed nearly two decades of garrison life between the wars—one of the few such stretches in it bloody history. By 1922, it was at Fort Benjamin Harrison near Indianapolis where it conducted CMTC courses, sometimes maneuvering at Fort Knox near Louisville on the Ohio River. During the great flood of 1937, it did yeoman service for the city there.

In early 1918, the 10th Infantry Regiment had been moved from the Panama Canal—which it had been guarding since war broke out in 1914—back to the States where its members were divided into cadres and sent out to become the nucleus of new regiments being formed at various stations. These regiments built upon the shoulders of 10th men saw service on all fronts in Europe. The 10th Regiment, refilled with new personnel, guarded munitions and key industries, and was engaged in strike duty until the end of the war.

During the years following WW I, the 10th performed garrison duty, trained civilian army components, participated in flood duty and summer field training until 1939.

The Fifth Gears Up For Another World War

At this point, the new Fifth, reorganized as a triangular type division, consisted of three infantry regiments—the Second, Tenth, and Eleventh Infantry; two Field Artillery regiments—the Nineteenth and the Twenty First; and divisional troops composed of the Seventh Engineers, Fifth Quartermaster Battalion, Fifth Medical Battalion, Fifth Signal Company, Division Headquarters, and a Military Police Company. (It should be noted here that during our American Civil War—around 80 years prior to this time—the 2nd, 10th, and 11th Infantry Regiments had comprised the Second Brigade at the famous Battles of Chancellorsville and Gettysburg).

It is also worth remarking here that the old World War I organization—the "heavy" or "square" type division—was larger and more cumbersome while this new "triangular" type which was smaller, could move faster and strike harder.

The first infantry units at Fort Custer, Michigan, which was to become the Division's permanent station, were drawn from the 2nd Infantry Regiment. The 10th, less two battalions, went from Fort Hayes, Ohio, to Fort McClellan on November 7, 1939, and the remaining two battalions went from Fort Thomas, Kentucky, to Fort McClellan three days later. The 11th, less the third battalion, moved from Fort Benjamin Harrison to Fort McClellan on November 10, 1939, with the remaining battalion coming south later that same month.

Brigadier General Campbell B. Hodges, the new Division Commander, took charge October 24, 1939. Then from July 17, 1940 through September 4, Brigadier General Lloyd R. Fredenhall commanded. At that date, Major General Joseph M. Cummins returned from the Panama Canal Zone to take charge.

The new Division's artillery regiments were the 19th which was activated as a 75mm gun unit of three battalions at Fort Knox, Kentucky on October 31, 1939; and the 21st which was activated as a 155mm Howitzer regiment of two battalions at Ft. Knox on October 6, 1949. They arrived at McClellan or January 25, 1939 and February 10, 1940 respectively.

Reorganization took place on October 14, 1940, as follows: Headquarters Battalion, Fifth Division Artillery, was organized from the HQ and HQ Battery of the 1st Battalion, 21st Field Artillery. The 21st was reorganized as a battalion with a HQ battery, three firing batteries, a service battery and a 75mm anti-tank battery. The 1st Battalion, 19th Field Artillery, was redesignated the 19th Field Artillery Battalion, the 2nd Battalion became the 46th Field Artillery Battalion, and the 3rd Battalion became the 50th Field Artillery.

Activated on October 7, 1939, the 7th Engineer Battalion, moved from Fort Logan, Colorado, to McClellan in October, 1939.

The 5th Quartermaster Battalion arrived at McClellan on November 4, 1939 from Fort Knox. The 5th Medical Battalion—redesignated the 4th on July 1, 1940, joined the Fifth Division on May 27, 1940. The 5th Reconnaissance Troop was brought to Fort Custer November 7, 1940.

The units in the new Fifth which were part of the original World War I Red Diamond division are worth mentioning here to emphasize continuity: the 11th Infantry Regiment, the 19th and 21st Field Artillery regiments, and the 7th Engineers all served with the Fifth in France in 1918. These units brought with them a tradition of pride and confidence to the newly reconstituted whole in 1939. The chain had remained unbroken during the uneasy peace between the two wars.

Training The New Fifth

In the fall of 1940, construction of the new barracks at Fort Custer continued apace, then General Cummins moved the Division Headquarters there December 19, 1940. Various units began to arrive soon thereafter and training went ahead at a faster clip. And although, of course, no one could know it, the assault at Pearl Harbor was less than a year away now.

The problem in this phase of the Division's reconstruction was the same as that in WW I—how to effectively train green Selective Service troops with the relatively small number of seasoned cadre.

Fort Custer, Michigan, home of the 5th Infantry Division in 1941. (Courtesy of William Colon)

Be that as it may, in the spring of 1941 a thorough inspection of the Fifth was made by Lt. Gen. Ben Lear, and it proved that the training program had been quite effective. His report to Gen. Cummins contained the following words:

"I want to congratulate you on the specially fine showing which your command has just made in the tests covering the 13 weeks of training under the Mobilization Training Program. The progress of the officers and enlisted men is highly satisfactory and shows they are well prepared for instruction under the combined training program. I anticipate splendid things from your Division."

This newly fledged unit of Red Diamond men was then ready to move out on a 600 mile march from Fort Custer to central Tennessee on May 20, 1941. Once there, it participated in maneuvers conducted by the Second Army from June 2 to 28. Even though there were more than 5,000 recent inductees in the unit, officers of the Second Army praised the Fifth Division's performance.

Early in July, the Fifth returned to Fort Custer. Then on July 24, Gen. Cummins was relieved of command by Maj. Gen. Charles H. Bonesteel—a man surely named to be a good soldier. And that was no doubt reassuring because the rumors of war were rife; to many, our entry into the European conflict seemed inevitable at this point. That we might be at war with the Japanese, as well, had a growing ring of credibility.

When Gen. Bonesteel took command, all available regular army officers had been recently shifted to the 10th Infantry and the 46th Field Artillery Battalion—to make a complete combat team. Then soon thereafter, Brigadier General Cortland Parker succeeded Gen. Bonesteel.

Late in August the Division was off again to Louisiana for more "war games" during which time the Fifth Anti-tank Battalion was formed; its personnel were drawn from the 21st Field Artillery Battalion and the three anti-tank companies. It was later designated the 605th Tank Destroyer Battalion.

When it left for Louisiana, however, the Division was minus the 10th Combat Team. It stayed behind, and for the Fifth this was the first hint of what fate had in store. The 10th was soon on the way to Iceland. Yes, Iceland—the very word still sends shivers through many veterans. And when the rest of Division returned to Fort Custer, it too began to ready itself for shipping out to Iceland. The movement would take months in a piecemeal fashion—the first arrived September 16, 1941, and last on May 10, 1942. The war was spreading quickly around the world, and it was time for the Red Diamond men to again say "We Will."

WORLD WAR II

Background To The War

Let us withdraw briefly here and sketch in the historical background up to this moment. The obvious question here is why was the Fifth reactivated, why this rigorous training, to what ominous call were the men in the Fort Custer barracks waking each day?

Scarcely a month before the Fifth was rejuvenated on October 16, 1939, the German army invaded Poland and what would become the greatest war in the history of mankind began.

September 1, 1939. Blitzkrieg! The little corporal of World War I was now the Commander in Chief of a great war machine, and it drove across the Polish border with ease. For a quarter of a century, Hitler had fought his way up the political ladder in Germany, and now he had his chance to avenge the Versailles Treaty. Among other things, the treaty had carved a Polish corridor out of Germany. Germany's brief experiment in democracy had failed, and one fateful opportunity after another had been seized by the National Socialist Party Hitler headed. In violation of the Versailles Treaty, he had openly rearmed his country, and his expansionist aims were obvious by the mid-1930s if one had simply had the foresight and courage to read them. In 1938, German tanks moved into Austria. Der Fuehrer shrilly threatened Czechoslovakia. The appeasing leaders of the west met at Munich and gave Hitler what he wanted—the Czech state was ruthlessly carved up in the name of "peace in our time," and would be under German domination until the Fifth Division participated in its liberation near the end of the war.

Next Hitler demanded the return of Danzig from the Poles as well as corridor access. He bullied little Lithuania to surrender Memelland. Rumania was forced to agree to let the Germans have its oil. The Germans and Italians under Mussolini lent military aid to Francisco Franco who finished the Spanish Civil War and the siege of Madrid on March 28. And thus Fascism was rampant in Europe.

Then at 4:40 a.m. on September 1, the German air force began bombing Polish airfields all over the country. A German battleship opened fire on the Polish fortress at Danzig; the Nazi SS took control of the whole city, and by then German tanks were blitzing the borders in the north, south, and west—a new "lightning warfare" was afield when the sun rose that morning. The radios in the army barracks across American were abuzz that day, and that evening the headlines were big and bold.

By mid-1940—when the Fifth Infantry Division was at Camp McCoy, Wisconsin, practicing on field problems and marksmanship— France fell before the Nazi onslaught. No one thought that France would ever fall, but by then almost all of Europe was in German hands. England was now a much easier target from the air.

In Washington at this time, President Roosevelt was working overtime to help build a broad base of popular support for entry into the war. By July of 1941 when the first combat team of the Fifth Division was formed, the Japanese were poised in the Pacific.

The attack, of course, came on December 7, 1941, and we were caught unawares at Pearl Harbor. Our losses there were staggering, and the next day, President Roosevelt made his famous "day of infamy" speech to Congress and asked for a declaration of war against Japan and got it. Until that attack at

Honolulu, we had been torn with dissension and uncertainty. Nevertheless, units of the Fifth Infantry Division were already either in Iceland, enroute or preparing to go. And from that first day of war never had the US been so united. The recruiting stations were immediately full all across the nation. Young men who would help swell the ranks of the Fifth in the coming months were fighting mad.

Iceland

Why were we there? What mission took the Fifth Infantry Division to this huge remote island in the North Atlantic? It seems that by June 1941 the War Plans Division had undertaken a huge program to defend our hemisphere from the German threat. With U-boats already operating with virtual impunity in the Atlantic—both North and South—this was an important goal.

Now Iceland fell outside what was defined as our hemisphere, but it was crucial to our securing of the North Atlantic against the German navy. Consequently 20,000 British troops were stationed there by the middle of 1941, but the Icelandic government wanted them out. Would the Americans take their place? "We Will."

Iceland–the home of the Fifth in 1942-1943 (Courtesy of William Colon)

Iceland in 1942-1943 (Courtesy of William Colon)

And so by the spring of 1942, there were 15,000 American GIs there—largely our Fifth Infantry Division. And Iceland was at best a difficult place to defend even without an enemy in sight. The winters were blanketed in continuous darkness. The road conditions were poor, in fact, impassable nine months of the year except in the urban area of Reykjavik. What's more, the Division was spread so thinly it was virtually impossible to train in large units.

For the most part, the Fifth was used for coastal observation and patrol, for stevedore work on docks, and for building the huge Meeks airfield on Keflavik peninsula. Here's a 2nd Infantry Regiment trooper on his unit's work for the roughly 18 months the Fifth was there. We spent most of our time, he said, "*on an almost continuous schedule at the docks, unloading and loading supply ships. When the weather slowed the cargo boats, this GI went through defensive exercises—climbing up and down the jagged lava formations, through seep bogs and across the moss-covered tundra.*"

The famous 7th Engineers were also to find out some strange things about this place. The topsoil was lava ash packed firm in the cold climate and beneath it a substance like quicksand. If one of their bulldozers broke through that crust, it would quickly sink deep. And if the language problem weren't enough, the Icelandic inch was shorter than the American inch as the local carpenters and the Fifth's engineers also discovered when the former were set to building housing for the troops. The Nissen hut was just about the only type of building for the GIs—used for living quarters, day rooms, kitchens, mess halls, garages and hospitals.

The 2nd Inf. Regiment GI goes on, "*We endured the fickle antics of the climate by having one minute to push against sleet and snow driven in sharp, biting anger before a mile-a-minute gale—and the next minute being soaked to the skin by a frigid rain or teased by an anemic sun peaking over the edge of the world.*"

"*In the evening, the soldiers sat around their stoves, listened to the wind shriek, exchanged stories of the past, and wrote letters home.*" Now and then bored and lonely, they would "*stroll the streets in Reykjavik, watch the Icelanders who seldom if ever spoke,...and visit the Red Cross clubhouse—the one spark of the US—where they would play a game of pool, have some cakes and coffee,*" and then trudge back to camp.

Such was life in Iceland, however, the schooling and training the troops received here was to pay off in spades later. Commanders and staff acquired experience they would call upon later, especially since they were coordinating closely with the US Marines, Navy, and other branches as well as British forces. There was some winter warfare training. Not least in importance, this interlude gave the majority of the men who would do the foot slogging and hard-core fighting a chance to bond and knit together in an unbreakable way.

Then by the end of August 1943, the last of the Fifth had shipped out once again—this time for England which put them right across the channel from the enemy's guns.

Artillery crew of the 46th FA Battalion take up various positions at a forward observation post at Westdown Fields, Tidworth Wilts, England 2 October 1943. (National Archives US Army Photo)

England And Ireland

England and Ireland were to be the site of the training for the Fifth and vast numbers of more units in preparation for what many sensed would be—sooner or later—an invasion of continental Europe. The Fifth would reorganize and train in earnest in England until late October. Here, too, it was assigned—under V Corps—a section of the British coast to defend in case of an attack.

After first arriving in England and settling in at Tidworth Garrison, some much needed leaves, furloughs, and passes were given for the first time in nearly 18 months. The training which began soon emphasized the individual soldier, qualification in arms, and physical conditioning. Obsolete weapons such as the 37mm antitank guns were replaced by heavier 57mm weapons. 105mm howitzers were added. Combat equipment was issued. Artillery firing took place, and some unit exercises were executed with the British Home Guard.

And last but not least, the British "Land Army" girls needed assistance in harvesting crops since a majority of British men were on duty in the military. "We Will," said the Red Diamond men.

Then in late October, the Fifth moved to the mountains of Mourne in Northern Ireland. The men were billeted in small camps near the mountains, and here pre-invasion training would take place covering every phase of attack and defense. Problems involving larger and larger units were worked through until finally a division-wide exercise took them up the Slieve Donard peaks and some of the other mountains. The river crossings which had and would distinguish the Fifth in combat were practiced on small lakes complete with the engineers building and rebuilding bridges.

Artillery crew of the 50th FA Battalion prepares a 105mm howitzer for firing position while on maneuvers in England. (National Archives US Army Photo)

Here in Ireland, "Battle Drill," a system perfected by the British army was used so that every soldier knew by heart what his combat duties were. Every GI was to be proficient in more than one type weapon, and the Fifth poured tons of live ammo—including heavy artillery—into the sides of the Irish hills. Simulated combat conditions put men under the emotional stress they were soon to face. More than a thousand anti-aircraft gunners went through a special course.

Through the Irish fall and into the winter the intensive training went on. According to Albert Love and others, the widest range of skills were taught and practiced: scouting, patrolling, map and aerial photograph reading, first aid and sanitation, camouflage and concealment, junior office instruction, artillery fire adjustment, tank infantry cooperation, and so on—the Red Diamond men were put through their paces. They studied German weapons, equipment, and battle method. And finally, they were given a quick course in amphibious invasion since it had long since secretly been decided that the northern French coast was the main target for D-Day.

The drivers of the 5th Quartermaster Co. stand by their trucks just before they are ready to move out from Clough, County Down in Northern Ireland 8 March 1944. (National Archives US Army Photo)

Field artillery soldiers clean and work on their field pieces at the camp in Mourne near Kilkeal, County Down, Northern Ireland 13 March 1944. (National Archives US Army Photo)

Men of the Division Artillery participate in a demonstration of a landing by the infantry and engineers near Annalone, County Down 23 March 1944. (National Archives US Army Photo)

Lt. General G. S. Patton CO of the 3rd Army inspects the 816th Tank Destroyer Battalion attached to the 5th under his command in Greencastle, County Down on 30 March 1944. (National Archives US Army Photo)

Yes, June 1944 was drawing quickly near—and the largest amphibious assault in the history of human warfare. The invasion was called Operation Overlord, and from its inception in November of 1943 it was as secret and unreadable as humanly possible. It is miraculous that this was achieved when you consider its vast scope: by the end of June 6, 1944—after one day of horrendous fighting—57,506 American ground and 17,000 airborne troops as well as 75,215 British and Canadian troops were ashore and tenuously established. The numbers of air and sea craft, of support personnel, and so on has never before or after been equaled. And the eleven months between this famous date and Victory in Europe Day would encompass some the most outstanding moments in the Fifth Division's history.

The historian of the 2nd Infantry Regiment describes what was happening to the Fifth Division 23 days after the first Allied troops hit the beach at Normandy:

"*Training completed and equipment ready, the 2nd Infantry was alerted at 2400, June 29 for overseas movement. All personnel were 'sealed' in their barracks. No officer or enlisted man was permitted to leave without a pass signed by the Regimental Commander.*" One can easily imagine how the tension began to build at this point, the rumors, the speculation, the hopes and fears. "*The final plans for loading were made, and on July 5 and 6, the Regiment (and the rest of the Division) boarded army transports (12 Liberty ships) in Belfast Harbor and sailed at midnight on the 6th.*"

"*The voyage was a quiet one. Briefing of officers and troops was accomplished on the 7th and 8th, and on the 9th the convoy arrived off the coast of Normandy, due east of St. Mere Eglise.*"

There is a photograph taken on board one of the transports which shows the men stretched out on the deck in life jackets. Many are lying down and catching the sun and perhaps a nap. They know that where they are going there will be little sound rest for a long time. The Red Diamond men sit or lie close together, yet, at the same time, each seems in his own world. The faces are grave, concentrating. On all sides rose a forest of masts as transports, LCIs, LCVPs, and tank lighters scurried to and from the shore.

The 2nd Regiment's historian goes on: "*At 2205, the first 2nd Infantry troops landed on Utah Beach.*" Though they would be landing on "friendly beaches," you could hear the din of artillery in the inland distance. The Fifth Infantry Division was on its way into the fire. In a few days, the first Fifth Division life would be lost. There were Germans only 12 miles away, and their air attacks might come at any time.

The Fifth At Normandy

Once ashore, the troops of the Fifth were marched to areas of transit. All around them, according to Division historians, were "*tangled wreckage, barbed wire fences, and ever present 'Achtung Minen' signs*" warning of ground mines. Soon thereafter, the men marched 1 1/2 miles through dangerous dunes and hedgerows to the Division assemblage area west of Montebourg. They were assigned to the First US Army and in reserve until a Corps assignment was made.

The next day, the vehicles were unloaded and the men picked up the heavier equipment and duffle bags, and by the July 12 all the men and their gear were in one place. Several times during the previous nights German planes made reconnaissance and harassment runs over the Fifth, and this inspired adequate "digging in" as nothing else could.

Now assigned to V Corps, on July 12, the Fifth was ordered to relieve the First Infantry Division in the Caumont sector; relief was made unit for unit with no changes in disposition. Division movement was made on organic transportation plus six truck companies or around 290 trucks. Passing through the rolling farm country with its small fields and hedgerows, guides from the First met and warily led the Red Diamond men to their first combat positions.

Infantrymen are busy packing their supplies for loading onto a transport which will take them to the fighting front in France. (Courtesy of William Colon)

These vehicles are being driven ashore from an LST on the French coast on 13 July 1944. (Courtesy of William Colon)

The new troops heard their first incoming artillery at this time and the ominous swishing sound of the German 88s. They began to learn immediately how to make a foxhole in one leap. By 1400, the replacement was complete and the Fifth Infantry Division was in line for the first time in the war. Fortunately, some experienced NCOs and Officers of the First stayed beside the Red Diamond men to help break them in to their new situation.

As early as July 13, units of the 2nd Infantry had relieved the 16th Infantry Regiment, 1st Division. In these first few days in combat there was extremely heavy mortar and machine gun fire, sniper fire, and sharp encounters with enemy patrols all through the nights. And by midnight of the July 14, the first Red Diamond man had fallen. S/Sgt. Bass of Service Company was killed by shell fire and three others were wounded.

During that time, the troops had their first encounters with the German "Burp gun" or Schmeisser Machine Pistol's rapid fire sound, the "Screaming Mimi," and the use of smoke for concealment. They also became acquainted with the result of heavy French rains which they came to call "General Mud." Only a few roads were paved, and these were usually under artillery fire. Here they took their first prisoners—mostly young men with at least six months training. Six enemy planes were shot down. Numerous outpost and patrol fights piled up the first of many enemy dead to the Fifth's credit. In addition, the Division's patrol activity here helped compile information on enemy positions which would be crucial in the attack at Vidouville.

In various encounters with the enemy here, it became clear that his morale was high. The Germans were well-entrenched and well-organized including three Paratroop Regiments and 4 Paratroop Divisions plus a reconnaissance company.

For this first operation and many which would follow, the Fifth Infantry Division's three combat teams were composed as follows:

Second Combat Team. Second Infantry Regiment; 50th Artillery Battalion; Company A, 735th Tank Battalion; Company A, 818th Tank Destroyer Battalion; Company A, 7th Engineer Battalion; Battery C, 449th Anti-Aircraft Artillery Automatic Weapons Battalion; and Collecting Company A, 5th Medical Battalion.

Tenth Combat Team. Tenth Infantry Regiment; 46th Field Artillery Battalion; Company B, 735th Tank Battalion; Company B, 818th Tank Destroyer Battalion; Company B, 7th Engineer Battalion; Battery D, 449th Anti-Aircraft Artillery Automatic Weapons Battalion; and Collecting Company B, 5th Medical Battalion.

Eleventh Combat Team. Eleventh Infantry Regiment; 19th Field Artillery Battalion; Company C, 735th Tank Battalion; Company C, 818th Tank Destroyer Battalion; Company C, 7th Engineer Battalion; Battery A, 449th Anti-Aircraft Artillery Automatic Weapons Battalion; and Collecting Company C, 5th Medical Battalion.

A medic administers aid to a wounded soldier at Normandy in July of 1944. (Courtesy of Joseph G. Rahie)

In time it became clear that the enemy was strengthening his positions opposite the Fifth. Mines were being laid, trip flares set, obstacles were being constructed—in some ways at least, it was a bit like World War I in the trenches. The two new German units were pegged as the 9th Paratroop Regiment and the 2nd Panzer Grenadier Regiment. The Fifth's positions in the sector were unchanged until July 24 when the Scottish Division relieved the 10th and 11th Infantry Regiments.

At this point, the Fifth was under orders to take part in Operation Cobra—a breakthrough effort to initially be made in the St. Lo area, the major town and road center of the area, then to involve the whole First Army front. First, bombers "carpet bombed" the enemy on July 25th; then, on the 26th at 0635, the Second Infantry Regiment was ordered to "jump off."

The Normandy Breakthrough—The Battle Of Vidouville

"*Until now, we have been marking time. Now we were to go on the offensive,*" writes the 2nd Reg.'s historian, "*with two battalions abreast: the 1st Battalion on the right commanded by Lt. Col. Childs, the 3rd Battalion on the left commanded by Lt. Col. Lindley. Regimental objectives: to capture the town of Vidouville and to secure the high ground at Highway 3. Initially, the 2nd Battalion would remain in reserve.*"

And here is the first unit of the Fifth—the 1st Battalion, 2nd Regiment—in action: the 1st *"encountered intense sniper fire as it crossed the LD. Company A met stiff resistance in La Miletiere Woods from an enemy force estimated at company strength."*

"Assisted by tanks and artillery fire, Company A drove through the resistance leaving mopping up operations to its rear elements. Then enemy machine guns and automatic hand weapons opened up from close range and took heavy toll of our personnel. Pre-registered 88's covered the open ground to our front—the ground we were obliged to move over. Company A was finally stopped by sheer weight of firepower when within 100 yards of Vidouville."

The Regimental historian goes on: *"Company B ran into much the same sort of fight on the right flank. They originally drove through the woods but were stopped at its southern edge by a strong point which included an 88 concealed in a house at the edge of the clearing. Both companies suffered heavy casualties in killed and wounded, so Company C in reserve was committed in Co. A's zone of action—to attack and reduce the garrison at Vidouville."*

"Then Companies B and C resumed the attack after brief reorganization and drove close to the village in the south. Two platoons of Company F commanded by Lt. John Savage were pushed into the town to mop up only to suffer heavily at the hands of well-placed enemy artillery fire. Company G was sent to clear out the woods. Meanwhile, the 3rd Battalion had met less resistance at first and was able to reach a line running due east of the town."

And so this first full-tilt offensive raged on. The Red Diamond men were at last putting all their training to its severest test and it was paying off. The Boche had paid heavily in casualties. After fierce fighting all day, by 1600 the objective was ours—Vidouville and environs. It was later discovered that some of the German snipers were tied up in the trees of the woods. And from German documents it was learned that the 2nd Combat Team had opposed the 9th Paratroop Regiment, 3rd Paratroop Division. At a strength of two battalions, the Germans considered it their best unit in Normandy. This enemy had been well-dug in and dead-set against giving any ground.

Division historians report that as night fell, the 3rd Battalion, 11th Infantry Regiment, was shifted to the 2nd Infantry Division on Hill 192. Later, the rest of the 11th was moved there as well. Its 1st Battalion was ordered to prepare for attack in the morning. Through the night, the gun crews of the 21st Field Artillery caught cat naps after having supported the Division attacks all day. Both the 2nd Combat team and the Germans were preparing to begin the next day fighting. The Germans were very much at home and had fallen back to secure reserve positions. The Red Diamond men were new to this, and were just beginning to adjust to the stress of heated combat.

The next day—July 27—began with a heavy German 88m. artillery bombardment. By 1400, Companies B and E, 2nd Regiment, were on the attack, and through the day and night bitter fighting ensued. It soon became clear that the Germans intended to reclaim what they had lost the day before. All day they attacked and we countered. Their determination was strong, and the fighting went on into the night. Massed in strength in front of Company E, the Boche attacked yet again at 2005 hours and drove them back—collapsing our whole line. Again we rallied and pushed them back in turn. And so the night went like a nightmare.

During this night, the 10th Infantry Regiment was fast on its way to relieve the 9th Infantry Regiment of the Second Division. The 10th's 1st Battalion was moved into Division reserve near Montrabot Woods just 2000 yards behind the Red Diamond Second Combat Team.

Early the next morning, the Fifth was busy reorganizing and consolidating their positions. The dead were removed, and the wounded were given first aid and evacuated. Medical corpsmen did their much welcomed work. Re-supply was in order, but it had to be done under artillery and mortar fire. The 10th Combat Team moved forward a bit for a better position.

Then at 1800, Corps Command ordered the Fifth Division forward onto a ridge near an important road junction west of Vidouville. From there, the next objective would be the legendary Hill 183. The 2nd Regiment was ordered to stay in place, the 11th to stay in reserve behind the 10th which was to attack on July 29th.

On the morning of the 29th, the 10th's 2nd and 3rd Battalions led the assault with the 1st Battalion in reserve, and by 1520 they had successfully won all the ground leading up to Hill 183. Then their advance was slowed by heavy enemy fire as they began working their way up the lower slopes. Mortar, machine gun, and rifle fire poured down on them. In addition, sniper fire came from the rear and artillery fire increased. The 2nd and 3rd Battalions dug in; at this point, it was clear this hill was to be fiercely contested.

The Fifth had come up face to face with what Division historians describe as "*the ring of steel the Boche had hoped to forge around the hard-won Allied beachhead after the big invasion of June*." They had fought courageously their first two weeks in combat, and at sundown on the 29th, the 2nd Infantry Regiment held the Division's left sector, the 10th held the right. The 11th, being held in reserve, was ordered to back up the 10th which would attack the next morning. Major General S. Leroy Irwin, the Fifth's Commanding General, had received orders to push his men to the Vire River. Hill 183 stood before them.

July 30 at 0900, the 10th Infantry Regiment lined up in battle order—3rd Battalion on the left (K Company left, L Company right, I Company in reserve); 2nd Battalion on the right (E Company left, G Company right, F Company in reserve). And finally, 1st Battalion was held in reserve. The 10th immediately met withering fire and was then hit with a counterattack by 1030. The terrain itself made advancing doubly difficult. Small fields and thick hedgerows made easily defended obstacles in themselves. The counterattack smashed into L and E Companies and further into K and G. Casualties were quickly piling up, and the corpsmen themselves were fired on.

Tanks of Company B, 735th Tank Battalion were moved to support the 2nd Battalion's line. In addition, the 46th Field Artillery poured hot bombardment on the enemy, and around 1200 the counterattack began to lose momentum. The tanks were then moved to the 3rd Battalion, and a slow movement forward began at last. Even then, men in Companies K and L strode into a field of the infamous Schumines. But the 2nd and 3rd were forcing their way up Hill 183. The enemy fell back only when surrounded or outflanked.

Then, finally, the 3rd Battalion under Maj. A.P. Shipley reached the top of the hill. His men found an enemy mortar observation post in a tree which directly overlooked our line of departure—no wonder the 10th Combat team had taken such heavy fire. By 2100 all companies (K, L,& G with I and F in close support) were consolidating gains south of Hill 183, and the Fifth had made one of its first historic wins in this war.

Here is what it cost: 77 enlisted men and 1 officer killed; 323 enlisted men and 23 officers wounded; and 35 enlisted men missing. The enemy loss was estimated at 700 to 750. The new graves of 450 enemy were found the next day.

As the 10th had attacked Hill 183 to its left, the 2nd Combat Team had attacked across the Haut Vidouville-Caumont road. The 11th was then pushed to the fore in a night attack on July 31. They jumped off through the lines of the 10th at 0400, and when they met little resistance—except for Schumines—they began to pursue the enemy for 15 miles. They moved in two columns: the first composed of Cannon Company, and both a Tank Company and a Tank Destroyer Company. The other column was headed by 1st Battalion then Regimental Headquarters, 19th Field Artillery Battalion, a platoon of Tank Destroyers, the 3rd Battalion and Service Company trains. All the while, the Mine Platoon and a platoon of engineers stayed busy clearing the roads of mines and other obstacles.

This advance by the 11th was eventually slowed by enemy fire in the Le Pit area. Company B was trapped and pinned down by the Germans who had waited until we were at close range and in the open.

Company A came to B's aid—but they too were hit hard from another stronghold. Then Company G and tanks from C Company, 735th Tank Battalion assaulted the enemy's right flank and forced him to withdraw.

The 11th took 25 prisoners and a battery of booby-trapped 105m howitzers. The enemy had fought a skillful delaying action against an aggressive force of Red Diamond men who were now ordered to stop further advancement south.

The 2nd Combat Team continued to attack in advance guard formation. No other Fifth Division unit could be advanced due to the presence of two British armored divisions in the area. The 2nd Team moved from La Ferriere toward the Soulvevre River on August 1, and did not meet remarkable resistance up to the bridge which was held by a German platoon with machine guns and mortars. The First Battalion hit them hard and drove them out. 2nd and 3rd Battalions closed up in the rear and consolidated.

Meanwhile the 10th Combat Team was holding its position along the Forchet-La Morginere road south of Hill 183. The north bank of the Soulevere River was patrolled by the Fifth Reconnaissance Troop. At this time, the British 8th Armored Division was moved through the Fifth's zone, and necessitated it stay put.

It is hoped the detailed narrative of combat operations we have just finished will have given the reader a sampling of what life and death in the Fifth would be like for months to come. At every juncture, it was clear that intricate cooperation between all elements of each combat team was necessary for the Division's exceptional successes—and this in their first few weeks of fighting.

By August 2, all elements of the Fifth were concentrated near Aux Malles for a brief respite. Here they could bath and change battle stained clothes for the first time. Reorganization took place; searches for MIAs were made; citations were made; and hedgerow tactics were refined.

Looking back into July, the fighting Fifth could be proud of its first showing on French soil. It had broken through the "iron ring" of German resistance to the Allies' invasion. The troops they had faced were the enemy's best. The V Corps Commander gratefully commended them. Along with many others, they had played an important role in the famed "Normandy Breakthrough," and established a reputation for the new Red Diamond. Significantly, the Germans were routed and in retreat.

Fifth Joins Third Army

"*On August 4 we moved by motor to a concentration area near Cherency Le Heron, over black top roads in warm and clear weather for a distance of 51 miles—to become a part of the XX Corps*," writes the 2nd Infantry Regiment historian, and thus begins the Fifth Division's distinguished record as part of the Third Army commanded by the legendary George S. Patton.

With the Third Army, the Red Diamond men had an important role to play in many battles to come across northern France. At this time, the Allies were gathering their forces at Vitre—where the tongs of the Allies' deadly pincer movements were assembled. They would had to drive yet further toward Paris and beyond—against an enemy determined to hold his ground or fight costly delaying actions.

In every little village the Fifth Division and the other Allies passed through now, the French were turning out to show immense gratitude. Our men had the warm reception of a liberating army. They passed Avranches and Mont St. Michel. Each step forward from the coast by the Allies meant that much more French soil was free of oppressive German occupation.

Pushing to the Loire and Maine Rivers next, the Fifth had the objective of taking the town of Angers where the two rivers meet. On August 7th, the 11th Combat Team under Col. C.W. Yuill moved on Angers. At the same time, other units closed from the north and east under the command of Lt. Col. D.W.

Thackeray. These included the Fifth Cavalry Reconnaissance Troop; Co. C, 2nd Infantry; 81mm. Mortar Platoon, Co. H, 2nd Infantry; 1st Platoon, Co. A, 7th Engineers; a platoon of Clearing Company Fifth Medical Battalion; Co. D, 735th Tank Battalion; and elements of the Division Photo Team, the Military Interpretation Team and the Counter Intelligence Detachment.

This area contained a Gestapo HQ as well as a Naval Command Station where an underground radio center controlled the German Atlantic Fleet. In addition, the area lent the Germans access in retreat, thus, they were not expected to give up it easily.

By the night of August 7, the Task Force Thackeray reached Aze after some sporadic fighting which—among other things—cost us three tanks. There they spent the night and planned to continue their assault on Coubray in the morning but discovered on the 8th the enemy had withdrawn. They pushed forward southeast to Cherre and beyond meeting scattered resistance which grew more fierce as midday came.

Pushing on toward Chateau-Neauf-Sur-Sarthe during the afternoon, the Fifth had the enemy in retreat. The Task Force fortified the town and bivouacked there for the night. August 9 found them moving on southwest to take Le Lion where 500 SS troops had been earlier—and then on to take Champigne. At this point the Division Commander called for Task Force Thackeray to return to Division near Becon.

While Thackeray was making its advance, the 11th Combat Team was moving on Angers with orders to take it. The 1st Battalion, 10th Infantry outposted bridges at La Guerche De Britagne so the enemy could not destroy them in advance of our main force. The Reconnaissance and Intelligence Platoon also went ahead. They were assaulted four miles west of Angers, and Co. G—the advance guard—engaged the enemy the rest of the day and into the night so that they would not deter our main force.

The Battle At Angers

The Germans held a general line some one and a half kilometers from the city along which ran an anti-tank ditch and mine fields.

Boche marines were reported to be out blowing bridges and blocking roads, so the morning of August 8 at 0200 Co. I, 11th Infantry was ordered to cross the Maine River and secure the Loire River bridge south of Angers where they met with heavy fire. This began a series of fights through the day as the groundwork for the main assault on the town was being laid.

A fanatical company-strong suicidal enemy attack stands out in this preliminary jockeying for position. On August 9 at 0200 Co. K, 11th Infantry Team had crossed a crucial railroad bridge near Prunier which was the only link our forward troops had, and at 0300 the Germans came pouring down a slope with demolition charges strapped to themselves screaming "Kamerad;" these human kamikazes would explode themselves when they had been hit—trying to take out as many Americans as possible. Meanwhile, the Engineers were removing tellermines and a deadly boxcar which could have been exploded by the enemy.

Fighting throughout the night Companies K and L ran out of ammunition, and the big attack had to be put off from 0830 to 1015 the next morning after a 10 minute artillery barrage by the 19th Field Artillery and the Regimental Cannon Company. By noon, the 3rd Battalion's anti-tank platoon was crossing the bridge near Prunier to support the rifle companies should the enemy send tanks against them. The 10th Combat Team was taking positions in support of the 11th. The Red Diamond men were pouring over the railroad bridge as the attack continued northeast even though the bridge was often under heavy fire.

By 1715 on August 9, an insufferably hot day, Company I and K had taken the high ground which had been the key to the enemy's southern defense of Angers. That night, the bridgehead was consolidated, the wounded evacuated, and re-supply took place.

At 0900 on August 10, 3rd Battalion, 11th Infantry jumped off for its attack on Angers itself and to take the bridge over the Maine. The initial stiff enemy resistance grew hotter against our Companies E, I, K, and L. It was more like a street fight as they came to the city—with the Boche behind every house and wall. The light tanks of Co. D, 735 Tank Battalion, were effective in scaring up the securely entrenched and unrelenting enemy.

From 1300 to 2030, the Red Diamond men moved slowly and doggedly to cover the 2000 yards necessary to take the town. Finally then, the 3rd Battalion met with the 2nd and 1st Battalions, and the Boche by then were in full retreat—too fast for pursuit on foot. The 7th Engineers were already at work repairing the Maine bridge. Mopping up operations began.

Toward the southwest, we had advanced in the Empire area and near St. Gemmes Sur Loire and sent the Boche running there too, as well as east of St. Leonards and La Croix. On August 11 when they were taken, the battle of Angers was complete. Many enemy casualties had been inflicted, prisoners and key installations were taken as well as much abandoned enemy equipment and materiel.

A vitally important area, Angers was the first key victory for the Third Army in what would be a famous sweep forward from this date, and the Fifth Division had once again distinguished itself courageously taking the fight to the enemy and systematically routing him as the liberation of France continued.

Meanwhile, the 1st Battalion, 2nd Infantry had operated in the Nantes vicinity blocking the roads north of the city and preventing enemy troop movement to the north into the rear of the Angers area. It then was ordered to return to the Division where it aided in mopping up through August 11.

On August 12, the 2nd Combat Team organized a defense of Angers. The rest of the Division joined the 11th Combat Team 92 miles northeast near St. Calais. Such frequent moves were the rule rather than the exception it seemed, and the Division had by this time mastered striking their camp and being back on the road in something like an hour. Infantry rode on tanks, tank destroyers, anti-tank guns, captured vehicles, artillery trucks, and supply vehicles on these long stretches.

(As of August 13, the following units were no longer a part of the Fifth Division: 150th Engineer Combat Battalion; 537th Engineer Light Pontoon Company; Battery B, 7th Artillery Field Observation Battalion; 994th Engineer Treadway Bridge Company; 204th Field Artillery Battalion).

Chartres

The Germans were reported concentrating near Chartres at this time, and the Fifth was ordered to move once again in that direction. The 7th Armored Division spearheaded the drive toward Chartres and had met stiff opposition outside the town. Chartres had a population of 40,000 souls and was considered "The Gateway to Paris." The powers that be had decided that somehow the famous cathedral should be spared, and so our approach was geared to be "cathedral friendly." But first, the 2nd Regiment was alerted on August 17 to move north to take over the sector manned by the 7th Armored in the vicinity of Nogent Le Roi and mop up after it.

Then the Fifth moved northeast toward the famous town itself and met with small delaying action elements. The country side was flat and open, and they were thankfully out of hedgerow country.

On August 18, the Fifth got its orders to move on the city, and by 2200 the 2nd and 10th Combat Teams were in position east of Chartres.

The 7th Armored had initially breached the German defensive line and drove with tanks into the heart of the city, but then a fierce counter-attack from the Boche garrison drove them back out. It was then that the Fifth Division was ordered in to relieve them and take the town.

Taking a lion's share of the initial assault were the 2nd and 3rd Battalions of the 11th, the Regimental Cannon Company under Capt. Harry Smith. Later the 1st Battalion moved to city center from the east. Heavy howitzer fire by the Cannon Company hit on a German ammunition dump was a key turning point in a fight against a strong pocket of resistance. And soon thereafter, the whole Boche garrison surrendered to Companies E and F—more than 800 Germans were taken.

At Chartres the 11th lost four enlisted men, and one officer, plus 20 enlisted were wounded in two days of fighting.

Men of the 11th Infantry Regiment enter Chartres, France after driving the Nazis from the town 19 August 1944. (National Archives US Army Photo)

Notably, a plush German limousine along with much other military equipment was captured, and the car was presented to Gen. Patton by the 3rd Battalion. In addition, something like 50 ME-109s were destroyed at the German airport. The unique cathedral was fortunately saved for posterity.

On August 19, the 10th and 2nd Combat Teams consolidated their positions and completed mop-up operations. While the 11th occupied Chartres, the Fifth Cavalry Reconnaissance Troop set to work near Orleans to the southeast and Rambouillet (where they happened upon Mr. Ernest Hemmingway, an armed and fighting press man travelling with an armored patrol). Strong enemy forces were reported around Fontainebleau 60 miles east in which direction the Fifth was ordered to move on August 20th. It objectives would be Etampes 34 miles east, then Fontainebleau, then Montereau—72 miles.

The 2nd Combat team was responsible for taking Etampes. After hard fighting with the 1st and 3rd Battalions moving in on the north and the 2nd Battalion on the south, the enemy's delaying actions petered out, and the town was attacked in force on the morning of August 22 only to find little resistance. By 1030, all battalions were in town mopping up.

Moving toward Montereau, the 10th Combat Team met the enemy at Malesherbes where—crossing the Essone River—they took casualties while inflicting many more on the enemy. The unknowing French populace stood cheering Company L almost in the line of fire as the 10th took the town.

Meanwhile, the 11th Combat Team and the 2nd moved separately taking near areas as they went, including the town of La Chapelle where Companies K and L bore the brunt of the fight. K was under the command of Capt. John C. Dalton. Co. L was supported by tank destroyers and the anti-tank platoon on its flank as it drove to the town itself. Tank destroyers of Co. B, 818 Tank Destroyer Battalion penetrated the towns outer defenses, then Co. L arrived as K and I also attacked, and the Germans ran in full retreat before the Red Diamond men.

Three officers were killed and six wounded; six enlisted men were killed and 40 wounded. The mayor of La Chapelle presented the Battalion Commander Maj. Alden Shipley a Croix de Guerre he had won in 1939.

The Third Army's Historic Dash

Historians judge there has never in the history of mankind been as much movement of ground troops as there was in the month of August of 1944. The drive of the US Third Army—including our Fifth Division—from Avranches in Normandy to Lorraine is one of the epic stories of that historic August.

August 25, as Paris was finally liberated, the 4th Armored Division took Troyes on the upper Seine River. Our Fifth Infantry Division captured Fontainebleau that same day. Thus, according to historian Geoffrey Perret, General Patton's Third Army had "*the bridgeheads it needed to drive beyond the Seine southeast of Paris for an advance on the Meuse River.*" The Third Army's "*dash*" was under way.

The image of General George S. Patton leading his Third Army across France is one of the most stirring of World War II. And the men of the Fifth Infantry Division are part of that legend. The Third Army infantryman respected and loved and were endlessly inspired by their General.

Capt. Jack Lynch, 10th Combat Team, 2nd Battalion, recalled a speech Gen. Patton gave the Fifth at Kilkeel, County Down, Northern Ireland in January, 1944. That "*speech helped sustain us across France, the Rhine, and into Germany. I still like to think of us,*" he wrote after the war, "*as 'Patton's Kilkeel Commandos.*" And, of course, there were many speeches and orders and commendations and words of gratitude to come from the General once the Third Army was in France.

"*To be Patton roaring across France, scattering a beaten foe, was to feel more like a god than a man,*" writes Mr. Perret. His men captured the champagne caves at Rheims where the Germans were stopped in May 1918. In addition, there is the historic significance of the Third Army's capturing "*the forest of Argonne and the brooding battleground of Verdun.*" Some of that territory, of course, had been hallowed with Fifth Division blood in World War I as we saw earlier.

And yes, *"As Patton's armor rolled on toward the Meuse, it seemed as unstoppable as a force of nature."* But of course for the typical Red Diamond soldier, the "dash across France" was not as much like an athletic event as that phrase may sound. Capt. Lynch speaks for many when he says that although the media may have focussed on the tanks sweep across France, *"it was the infantry in trucks that went 70 miles a day and—from the breakout at St. Lo, in the Operation Cobra to the Moselle River and the Forts at Metz— about 600 miles altogether."*

Capt. Lynch even speaks of his personal dislike and dread of fighting with armored units because—among other reasons—they were so easily spotted and drew more enemy fire. However, in the balance, we had best conclude that the infantry and the armored made a great winning team—each coming to aid the other as the cooperation of the 7th Armored and our Fifth Division proved. Was it not because of Gen. Patton's potent combination of armor and infantry that the Third Army was unstoppable?

The Seine Crossed At Fontainebleau

Returning to our narrative now, the 11th Combat Team—with the 5th Cavalry Reconnaissance Troop and Regimental Intelligence and Reconnaissance Platoon out front—moved on Fontainebleau with its bridge over the Seine on August 23. Firmly entrenched on the opposite bank of the river, the Germans blew the bridge just before our recon unit arrived. (They had done this all along the Seine south of Paris). It fell to the Fifth Division here to construct and secure a crossing for the great sweep east.

Lt. Col. Kelley B. Lemon, 11th Infantry, 2nd Battalion Commander, made a legendary swim across the river under small arms fire to secure five small boats on the German side. Co. G. was the first to cross under the heroic leadership of Capt. Jack Gerrie and Platoon Sgt. Dupe Willingham. A medium tank was called in to cover for the crossing in the boats and canoe Gerrie had procured.

Heavy fire was trained on the 11th men by now—as Co. F also came across the river, then E and Battalion HQ attachments.

These troops dug in to defend their bridgehead, and it is well they did because the enemy would repeatedly try to drive them back into the river. Counterattacks followed one after another into the night. The 11th's Cannon Company successfully destroyed and dispersed enemy reserves, otherwise it is quite possible the enemy might have prevailed. It was also learned later that reinforcements were on the way—the Germans knew quite well how valuable this crossing would be.

Co. A had crossed by daylight, then Co. K at 0900 on August 24. Co. K then succeeded in taking the right flank high ground. A treadway bridge was

A US tank continues to roll forward toward Fontainebleau, France, as Fifth infantrymen fire at enemy troops across the Seine River 23 August 1944. (Courtesy of William Colon)

Tanks and infantrymen enter the town of Fontainebleau in August of 1944. (Courtesy of William Colon)

constructed by Co. C, 7th Engineers and 537 Engineer Light Pontoon Company. Immediately then, the tanks, tank destroyers, and artillery could pour across—as well as the rest of the 11th Team. In heavy rain and under fire which included light and heavy enemy artillery, the 11th Team had accomplished its objective with many casualties. The first bridgehead on the Seine was in place and well defended.

As Division commanders studied their maps, they could see that to the east France is criss-crossed by many more rivers. In fact, the further east you go—toward the Vosges and the Alps—the more streams and rivers there are and the deeper they get. The treadway bridge the 7th Engineers and the Pontoon Company laid out was the key to this "historic dash" for the armored would have otherwise been stalled again and again.

Gen. Patton had learned from his military history that armies often lost because they stopped in the evening at riverside only to be defeated by a revitalized enemy the next morning when they tried to cross. Therefore, as often as possible the treadway bridges went up and the Third Army went across before it ever laid down to rest.

The importance of the bridge was demonstrated yet again at Montereau where French partisans led members of the 10th Combat Team S-3 to three bridges the Germans intended to blow at any minute. Maj. Harris Walker's unit found five 1000-pound bombs lying on the main bridge, and they were removed by the Anti-tank Company Mine Platoon. But again, the Germans did not give up this area easily at all. Sixty-two enlisted and one officer were killed or wounded in the process.

Here, also, a Red Diamond man won the Congressional Medal of Honor—he was Pvt. Harold A. Garman, Co. B, 5th Medial Battalion. He was cited for his exceptional heroism at the Division's Montereau bridgehead—specifically the 10th Regiment's forced crossing of the Seine where Pvt. Garman saved the lives of three of his comrades. In a photograph showing Gen. Patton presenting the award, one sees that Pvt. Garman was a small wiry man, in fact, the General towers above him. As we quote from the official citation then, picture a man whom you would not likely take to be a hero should you meet him on the street, unless, of course, you could look into his brave heart.

"*Casualties were being evacuated to the southern shore in assault boats paddled by litter bearers from a medical battalion. Pvt. Garman, also a litter bearer, was working on the friendly shore carrying the wounded from the boats to waiting ambulances.*"

"As a boatload of wounded reached midstream, a German machine gun suddenly opened fire from a commanding position on the northern bank. All of the men in the boat immediately took to the water except one man who was so badly wounded he could not rise from his litter. Two other patients who were unable to swim because of their wounds clung to the side of the boat. Seeing the extreme danger of these patients, Pvt. Garman without a moment's hesitation plunged into the Seine."

"Swimming directly into the hail of machine gun bullets, he rapidly reached the assault boat and then—while still under accurately aimed fire—towed the boat with great effort to the southern shore. This soldier's moving heroism not only saved the lives of the three patients but so inspired his comrades that additional assault boats were immediately procured and the evacuation of the wounded resumed."

Pvt. Garman's "*conspicuous gallantry and intrepidity at the risk of his life above and beyond the call of duty*" are emblematic of the service of many Fifth Division medical corpsmen and other service personnel. Their work was essential to the infantryman's success, and they are not lauded enough in our history.

When Montereau and vicinity were finally secured by August 27, Division historians write that "*the way was opened for the Allied Armies to cut Paris off from the south, and to continue encirclement of the city and its suburbs by driving north from the Fifth Division's Seine River bridgeheads.*" For its performance at Montereau, the 10th Combat Team was awarded a unit citation by the Division Commander and a Letter of Commendation Gen. Patton.

Meanwhile, the 2nd Combat Team was establishing another bridgehead south of Montereau on the Yonne River at Misy Sur Yonne on the August 25, and then again at Nogent—and so it went for the Fifth all through this area.

At this point, the Fifth might have been chosen to help take Paris but that did not happen. Instead, the Red Diamond men were ordered to circle the city and continue sweeping northeast as the Third Army penetrated central France. Division historians write of the media's amazement as the infantry not only kept pace with the armor, but sometimes even passed it—at any time "*ready to dismount and drive the enemy from it prepared defenses, mopping up the areas left behind by the swift advance of tanks, establishing bridgeheads, and taking town after town as the bewildered German armies fell back to avoid complete encirclement.*"

On August 29, the move on Rheims by the 2nd Team began, and fortunately the town was not heavily defended. The high ground was taken from the retreating enemy, and early on August 30 the town was entered and more or less secured by noon. More than 300 Germans prisoners were taken here, and the 2nd Team's 3rd Battalion occupied the town.

August 31 found the 11th Combat Team moving out for Verdun 72 miles due east. Following the 7th Armored, they moved through the Argonne forest area where many Fifth Division men died in another war. At Verdun they found one bridge intact over the Meuse—the river which had figured so importantly in earlier Red Diamond history. The 1st Battalion, 11th Team, was ordered to take the high ground above this hallowed and haunted city—but later this fell to the 2nd Battalion. Here, the troops found much evidence of WWI everywhere in the vicinity.

The story goes that in nearby Langres Gen. Patton even found the same old man beside a manure pile where he had been 26 years ago when Patton was there. And there was Patton's old billet in Madame de Vaux's chateau in Bourg. In Chaumont there was Gen. Pershing's old headquarters where in a tiny office by the gate of the barracks Patton had located "*the seat of my first considerable command*" —that of the Headquarters troops.

By August 31, a bridgehead had been established across the Meuse. And so at this point, it was natural that Gen. Patton —and some in the Fifth Division—were at moments preoccupied with the past as they haunted these old battle fields—and looked ahead to driving into Germany itself.

August was over—and an unparalleled month of Third Army advancement across France. Over 175 miles had been driven through in just the last five days. The blitzkrieg tactics the Germans had created and perfected had been used against them with consummate military art. Historians note that after the surprise at Normandy and the break out, the Germans were never able to reestablish effective communication or coordination. Thus, their defense plan never had the careful organization it would have taken to even begin to stop the Allied onslaught. And now Patton's spearheads were at the Moselle. Nancy was within his grasp. Gen. Walton Walker's XX Corps was moving irresistibly toward Metz.

Nancy had never been fortified, but Metz was deemed by many to be impregnable. A network of 24 forts surrounded it. According to Ladislas Farago in his biography of Patton, these fortifications "*ranged from strong-points to major installations, formidable ...like the Jeanne d'Arc and the Driant works on the outskirts of Metz.*" He goes on: "*In the light of the ease with which France had been cleared, Metz was not expected to represent any real threat. Then, just when it seemed Metz, like Verdun, would fall, things took an unexpected turn. During the next two and a half months, the city came to epitomize the difficulties and hardships the Third Army had to endure as its big parade turned into a desperate slugging match.*" (One understands what he means even as "parade" rings untrue).

On August 31, Gen. Walker's XX Corps literally ran out of gas—only 35 miles from Metz on the Moselle. On his north flank, the 90th Infantry Division at Rheims was out of gas as well. The 7th Armored and our Fifth Division "*could make the last few miles to the Meuse only by siphoning fuel from the supply and transport vehicles,*" notes Mr. Farago. In short, the Third Army was stopped in its tracks just when reconnaissance was telling Gen. Patton he might keep plunging straight ahead at will. The General was fuming, and the frustration among the Red Diamond men was killing.

For five fateful days, the Third was out of gas. Historians speculate that this delay may have cost many thousands of lives in many battles that would not have otherwise been necessary. More bad news was that intelligence had very little hard information about the intricate fortifications of this pre-Roman city of Metz. It was well camouflaged in addition to the natural foliage which made aerial viewing next to impossible.

American infantrymen take a boat down to the banks of the Moselle River at Donot, France, to be used in taking them across to the city of Metz 8 September 1944. (Courtesy of William Colon)

Medics from the 2nd Battalion, 10th Infantry in a rare relaxed moment in France. Starting with smiling soldier on left in circle are soldiers Courtney, Whalen, Vest, Bartelt, C. Corbin, and giving "V" sign is Schwarts. Bersick is sitting by tree. Medic with Red Cross on Helmet is Denim. E. Corbin has hand on his head, and Tomicheck is sitting by tent. Standing reading paper is McKee. (Courtesy of M.F. Bartelt)

Metz And Fort Driant

By September 4, a modest flow of gasoline was underway, but where there had been no significant German forces in the path of advance five days before, now it was a different story. Where there had been bridges, now they were no more. Five Cavalry task forces feeling their way around Metz all meet with fierce resistance. In fact, elements of two German Corps now stood in a 180 mile front along the Moselle. The Germans had regarrisoned Metz with two divisions, a machine-gun company, an artillery battalion, and so on. It was ready for whatever the Americans threw at it.

And throw themselves at it, the Americans did. General Patton admitted later that his decision to run the Fifth Division against Fort Driant was one of two operations he regrettably described as a errors on his part. He was convinced the Driant group of forts could be taken by an aggressive frontal assault even though they put the Fifth at every disadvantage.

According to Mr. Farago, the fortifications "*stood on a tall hill,...enclosed by dense barbed wire, bisected by moats and ringed by concrete machine-gun emplacements and armored observation posts.*"

The central fort was "*surrounded by a water ditch, and five batteries, four inside the fort proper (with six 100mm. and six 150mm. guns; and one, the so-called Moselle Battery of three 100mm. guns just outside the enclosure. Permanent infantry trenches zigzagged through the fort, and thousands of feet of communications tunnels ran underground....*" And the awesome description goes on.

Col. Charles Yuill, 11th Combat Team commander, and Gen. Walker convinced Gen. Patton to let Yuill storm this fort with one battalion to test its strength on September 27. In this four hour assault which could not penetrate the interior, two infantry companies suffered 18 casualties. Nevertheless, both Col.

Yuill and Gen. Walker were now ready to mount a full-scale attack. Our Fifth Division Commander General Irvin at this point stepped in to object to the plan. (It is interesting to note here that Gen. Irwin, a West Point graduate of 1915, had been made the Fifth's commander when the Division was in England because he had so impressed Gen. Patton as the 9th Division's artillery commander in Tunisia).

Gen. Irwin's objections and those of Gen. Gay fell on deaf ears, however, and the Fifth was ordered to begin "*simultaneous preparations for subsequent attacks on the other forts at Metz as well.*" The attack on the fort jumped off October 3 in bad weather and with weak air and artillery support. In spite of all odds, Co. B of the 11th Regiment fought its way into the fort. However, by nightfall it was clear no permanent breach could be made at this time.

Floyd Fraley (left) and Dean Wakeland of Co. M, 2nd Infantry in Metz. (Courtesy of Joseph Rahie)

Afterwards—over repeated objections from Gen. Irwin. Gen. Patton ordered Gen. Walker to "*take Driant even if it took every man in XX Corps.*" And Mr. Farago quotes him as follows: "*I cannot allow an attack by this army to fail.*" By October 9, it had—for the time being—done just that. In spite of the Fifth Division's heroism, the system of forts did seem invulnerable. And by the night October 12-13, the Fifth was withdrawn after nine days of dogged persistence. This decision was warranted because there was not a sufficient force available and further attack, according to Division historians, would result in needless loss of life.

At the time of withdrawal, the situation of Col. Yuill's men "*both above and below ground had become...acute. Water was at a premium, rations and ammunition were replenished with great difficulty. It was virtually impossible to remove the dead and wounded owing to the fury of artillery and mortar fire around the barracks and on the positions of the attackers topside.*"

In armchair evaluations of this operation, it is usually pointed out that in addition to the advantage of the impregnable fort, the American artillery was limited to a few tubes per day and thus could not blast any opening to speak of. In addition, the Germans were for the most part fresh, while the Third Army was exhausted after its cross-country blitz. In fact, frustrated and hating to give up the offensive, Gen. Patton himself took a day off to rest now for the first time in this campaign.

Enemy losses at Driant were impossible to estimate though they were many. The Fifth's casualties were: 60 enlisted men killed in action, 527 wounded and 183 missing; 4 officers killed in action, 20 wounded and 4 missing. What a sacrifice of Red Diamond men!

The Fifth continued to play a major role in the fighting in the Metz area, and by November 8, Patton was given permission to take the offensive again. With the Fifth, the 90th Division and the 10th Armor made a double envelopment of the city, then the 95th went in to take it from 15,000 Germans. It took countless small infantry-artillery team actions to beat them down, then finally the city was considered officially captured November 21. In the endless Third Army fighting in the Metz area, 30,000 Germans were taken prisoner, and around 80,000 had been killed or wounded.

After a conference with the German commanders, Major John Acuff, Executive Officer of 3rd Battalion, 11th Infantry Team accepted the surrender of the large Verdun forts on November 26.

Following the surrender, Company K was cited for heroism at the Dornot bridgehead and had the honor of raising the flag over the fort. The Second Combat Infantry Regiment then relieved the 95th Infantry Division in the mission of containing the four forts which were still holding out.

On November 25, Gen. Patton drove into Metz to review what Mr. Farago calls "*the city's conquering heroes, the dog-tired officers and men of Gen. Irwin's workhorse Fifth Division.*" Gen. Patton's address to them included: "*It is needless to point out to men like you the pre-eminent value of disciplined valor. You have demonstrated your courage.... I am proud of you. Your country is proud of you. Your deeds in the battle for Metz will fill the pages of history for a thousand years.*"

The Battle Of The Bulge, Luxembourg City, And Echternach

After the Metz blood letting, we are at the beginning of December, and the Red Diamond men as well as the Third Army in general were decimated and tired. Gen. Patton was doing anything to drum up replacements including retraining 5,000 men from non-fighting slots. Slogging toward the German "West Wall" in early December, our troops were exhausted, wet, and cold. Nevertheless, the 10th Infantry Regiment was attached to the 95th Infantry Division and set on the attack east to the Saar River.

A bright note in this din is that on December 8 our 2nd Infantry Regiment received the surrender of Fort Driant where it fought so courageously in October.

Later the rest of the Fifth joined together again to fight at Saarlautern, then they were hurried north to Luxembourg to meet the Germans' vicious Ardennes offensive of December 16. Out of heavy fog, forty-one Boche divisions supported by 1,500 tanks and assault guns had attacked in an area where Intelligence experts had claimed this would be impossible. At last, the Germans were on the counter-offensive.

In brief, with the 6th German Panzer Army on the right, the Fifth Panzer in the center, and the Seventh Army on the left, the attack was to drive through the Ardennes Forest in Luxembourg and Belgium with the Sixth Panzer reaching the Meuse on the third day and crossing it on the fourth. Hitler was taking the biggest risk he could take. He would regain the initiative if he succeeded. In a famous order by Germany's Field Marshall Gerd von Rundstedt to his troops, he admitted that "*you know that all is at stake.*"

A forty-two day battle which Winston Churchill dubbed the Battle of the Bulge had begun.

Miraculously, the German attack of 200,000 men was a surprise which overran one American unit after another where their disposition was generally thin. Meanwhile, our 2nd and 11th Regiments were fighting well and pushing through the Siegfried Line in Saarlautern. Then Gen. Omar Bradley, commanding the 12th Army Group, decided to send the Third Army up to attack the south flank of the German offensive. To protect Luxembourg City and relieve the reeling 4th Infantry Division, Gen. Patton called on our Fifth.

5th Division troops don makeshift snowsuits for the Battle of the Bulge. (Courtesy of Joseph Rahie)

And in less than 22 hours, our 2nd Infantry Team had moved 100 miles through foul snowy weather and provided the called-for relief. An astonishing 80% of the Fifth was in the relief area in 24 hours. The whole Third Army, in fact, made an incredibly swift swing to the north. The Fifth's assignment was to strike the aggressors south flank and throw them back across the Sauer River near Echternach, and thus keep Luxembourg City from falling into their hands. And 48 hours after they had been first ordered to move out, our 10th Combat Team—attached to the 4th Division—was attacking.

Here is a Co. F., 10th Infantry Regiment Sergeant on the 2nd Battalion's advance near the Michelshof-Scheidgan road where successive barrages of shells exploded in their midst: "*It was so terrible, it was unbelievable. Even on the Moselle and at Pournoy we'd had foxholes. In the woods that day there was no place to take cover. Absolutely no way to escape the tree bursts. We even took the Kraut's foxholes, took'em with bayonets and rifle butts. You could hear the telephones of the forward observers ringing—they were so close, and they must have called that fire right down on their own heads.*"

"*In the first few minutes, we had lost three of the platoon leaders and only God knows how many men. When we finally drew back to reform, we were in bad shape. We'd started the attack with 140 men, and we had 46 present at roll call.*"

Snowcapped infantrymen advance across open ground at the Bulge. (Courtesy of Joseph Rahie)

"*In the final analysis,*" Mr. Farago suggests, "*it may be just a myth that the Battle of the Bulge was WON by Patton's Third Army.*" But "*by the remarkable incident of its defender's courage, Bastogne became the pivot on which—at first by accident and then by design—the entire enterprise turned from its beginning almost to its end.*" And it was Patton's counterattack to relieve Bastogne which marked this turning point in the Battle of the Bulge. He had two divisions moving toward Echternach—including our Fifth—to strengthen the southern shoulder of the Bulge, and three moving to hold the line from Echternach to Bastogne. The relief of the town itself was assigned to the 4th Armored Division.

Our 10th Combat Team was ordered to attack south of Echternach passing through elements of the decimated 4th Infantry Division. Then on the morning of December 24, our 2nd Infantry Reg. was ordered to relieve the hard-hit 12th Infantry, 4th Infantry Division. Meanwhile, the mission of our 11th Infantry Regiment was to cover the formation of the XII Corps near Luxembourg City.

In summing up the key role our Fifth's three combat teams played at the Bulge, Division historians point out that the German offensive toward Luxembourg City "*was abruptly halted, and the Fifth Division had advanced six miles in as many days in the face of heavy artillery, very heavy nebelwerfer and rocket fire, and sporadic airplane bombing and strafing. The Division had thrown two German divisions into utter confusion, recaptured much American equipment, and taken 830 prisoners. It had killed a much large number, eliminated the threat of the southern salient, and thrown the enemy back across the Sauer River—eliminating its bridgehead.*"

Gunners of Battery A, 19th FA Battalion near Haller, Luxembourg are in position with shells ready for rapid firing of a 105mm howitzer 12 January 1945. (National Archives US Army Photo)

Soldiers of the 11th Infantry Regiment moves into position in the line near Gralinger, Luxembourg on the US 3rd Front 22 January 1945. (National Archives US Army Photo)

Near Bollenadorf, Germany men of Co. B, 91st Chemical Battalion operate a 4.2 mortar to cover the troops of the 5th Division crossing the Sauer River 8 February 1945. (National Archives US Army Photo)

A half-track moving through two columns of infantrymen of the 2nd Infantry Regiment, 3rd Battalion, along a mountain road en route to Grevenstein, Germany in the Ruhr pocket 11 February 1945. (National Archives US Army Photo)

(l. to r.) Soldiers Cooper, Shefte, Herrin, Brooke, Bealer, Breachka, Randall, and Waddell in Hungerhof, Luxembourg 10 February 1945. (Courtesy of Byron Brooke)

The Third Army had relieved Bastogne, the massive German drive had been stopped, and the "Bulge" was slowly being pushed back into the Siegfried Line from which it emerged with such fanatical fury.

In one month, the Germans had seen the equivalent of 20 full-strength divisions, including equipment, destroyed. Hundreds of thousands of their dead and wounded troops, and the vast number of artillery pieces and tanks they had lost would be sorely missed as they tried to defend the Rhine.

No one could know, of course, but the war would be over 100 days after the Bulge.

The 5th Infantry Division bridge across the Sauer River into the Siegfried Line. (Courtesy of Joseph Rahie)

Crossing The Rhine

All along, Gen. Eisenhower's plan had been to bring all his armies up to the Rhine—for 450 miles from Switzerland to the North Sea. Field Marshall Montgomery would line up in northern Germany with 25 divisions, and Gen. Bradley with 36 divisions would take the southern line and breach the German defenses there. Gen. Bradley's "Lumberjack Plan" called for his First and Third Armies to move across the river in a huge pincer movement. Mr. Perret points out he intended to "*clear all German forces west of the Rhine from Dusseldorf down to Koblenz, roughly 75 miles away.*" Then the First and Third "*would link up somewhere in the vicinity of a small river-side resort called Remagen, 25 miles north of Koblenz.*"

So Patton was attacking once more—moving on Koblenz and the Rhine with his three corps. But first his XX Corps with our Fifth Division had cleared the Saar-Moselle triangle. Then on March 13, the Third Army began to cross the Moselle. Patton's thrust was slow at first through rough terrain, but then it quickly achieved breakneck speed. Showing his usual boldness, he sent our Fifth Division straight east at the Rhine. Here is Mr. Perret's over view of the crossing: "*At 10:30 pm on March 22, the division's 11th Infantry Regiment started crossing the river at Oppenheim, 10 miles north of Mainz. The Fifth Division had made more than twenty successful river crossings; it could improvise one even in the dark. In less than two hours, the entire regiment had crossed. By 10:30 the next morning all of the 5th Division's combat troops were on German soil; the 90th Division was starting to cross; and tanks were already clanging along a 1,000 foot treadway bridge spanning the river.*"

This was the first assault crossing of the Rhine in modern history, and it had been done, as the Third Army liaison officer reported: "*Without benefit of aerial bombardment, ground smoke, artillery preparation, and airborne assistance....*" And here is the Division historian's detailed description:

"*The Third Battalion's spearheading companies I and K moved down to the river bank where 204 Engineer Battalion personnel awaited in readiness. Preparations functioned quickly, smoothly, and above all quietly as assault teams were formed and loaded into boats. K Company shoved off at 2230 and paddled across the 800 foot river without a shot being fired from the enemy shore.*"

Infantrymen prepare to board trucks which will carry them to the Rhine River where they will continue attacks on the Germans 7 March 1945. (National Archives US Army Photo)

Men of the Headquarter Company, 2nd Battalion, 11th Infantry Regiment and vehicles move along the Moselle Bank opposite Maden as they advance on Lutz 15 March 1945. (National Archives US Army Photo)

"*In the first boat to reach the far bank were: Company Commander 1st Lt. Irven Jacobs, Lt. John Mannow, Pvt. 1st Class William Hewitt, Pvt. 1st Class Vergil Miller, Private Theodore Strategos, Pvt. Richard Huiller, Pvt. 1st Class Arthur Juengel, Pvt. John Surace, Technician Fifth Grade Richard Rose, and Pvt. John Paquitt. As Company K hit the far shore, a group of seven surprised Germans promptly surrendered and paddled themselves across the river unescorted.*"

Infantrymen and tanks pass through Castellaun, Germany 16 March 1945. (National Archives US Army Photo)

If only it had all been that easy. 1st Battalion was crossing 700 yards downstream, and Company B, 1st Platoon, was spotted by enemy machine gunners who opened up on them while still midstream.

This alerted the Germans along the entire regimental front, and when Company L, Third Battalion was crossing 10 minutes later they were paddling under intense fire and some infantrymen were wounded. This fighting which went on through the day and night was, of course, the most difficult challenge of the crossing, but the Fifth was used to raw battle to establish a bridgehead. And much more went into this historic crossing: the G-4 function of coordinating the engineer work with the supply needs of the regiments was also a tough task. The engineers set records for speed, building Class 40 rafts and two bridges—a heavy pontoon and treadway. The Navy too did its part with its LCVPs always on the move back and forth. The Quartermaster Company ceaselessly shuttled supplies and removed the wounded. Military police had to control the traffic over the bridges. In short, it was a division wide team effort. All this took place while German aircraft and artillery did its best to interfere.

The Fifth crossing the Rhine River at Nierstein 23 March 1945. (Courtesy of Joseph Rahie)

The Fifth crossing the Rhine River at Oppenheim over a bridge constructed in half a day. (Courtesy of Joseph Rahie)

And already our 1st Battalion, 11th Infantry was pushing on through Dornheim, Geinsheim, and Wallerstadten on its way to Berkach; in addition, the 1st Battalion, 2nd Infantry arrived and took Astheim. Then the German's most fierce attempt to displace the Fifth's bridgehead was launched. What they didn't know, though, was that 3rd Battalion, 11th Infantry was occupying the town of Trebur. The Red Diamond men had a furious fight on their hands there, and, at Astheim, as the night went on. There was street fighting in darkest conditions. The Fifth fought with spirit and prevailed. And when the melee was over, 300 enemy were dead and 200 taken prisoner. Miraculously, American casualties were light.

Frankfurt-Am-Maine

So the Fifth was well established on German soil at last. At the time, it was estimated the enemy had enough of what it takes to fight for perhaps a year. He was facing a powerful new Red Army drive from the east, yet his propaganda machine in some astonishing way was still able to keep his hope pumped up.

By March 26, the 10th Regiment was ready to cross the Main and enter Frankfurt, one of Germany's larger cities. The 1st Battalion jumped off from Nauheim and by 1350 hours Company C reached the large Rhine-Main Airfield which was probably the second largest in the country. A strong stand was made later by an SS unit against Companies B and C on this side of the Main. Then our 3rd Battalion, 11th Regiment—which had been held in reserve—was given the nod to hit the Frankfurt bridge site. Company K then had the honor of crossing the river into the city—as it had been first at the Rhine.

Companies K, L, and I set to work establishing a bridgehead under heavy bombardment. It may be that this bridge was the most threatened by heavy German artillery as any the Fifth encountered in its many bridge battles. The anti-aircraft guns which had once defended the airfields were turned on the Red

Soldiers advance cautiously in street fighting in Frankfort 27 March 1945. (National Archives US Army Photo)

Diamond men. All their battalions were targeted as they crossed. Once across, Col. Roffe's 2nd Regiment led the way in clearing the city of opposition, and by March 30, the city was Red Diamond territory.

At this point, the Fifth Division had been ceaselessly on the move since November 1, 1944. It was due a much needed rest, and thus it went into XX Corps reserve; then as the fighting blew past Frankfurt, it went into Third Army reserve, then SHAEF reserve. The men at last had a chance to relax, to clean up, and actually sit down to a decent meal.

(The weary 2nd Regiment was an exception, though, since it had to take off again from March 31 to April 5 to help quell an SS Division which had broken loose).

Now rumors—which always plague the enlisted man—rumors had it that the Fifth Division had fought its last, that the war was all but over. And although of course this was not the case, the Red Diamond man's morale was high as he gained strength through nights of uninterrupted sleep and enjoyed the sights of the city in spite of its bomb damage.

The Ruhr Pocket

By April 5, our 11th Regiment in reserve had been appointed to be the "palace guard" of the advance command post of the Supreme Headquarters, Allied Expeditionary Forces (SHAEF), which was moving from France to Frankfurt. Meanwhile, the rest of the division was moving to reassemble in the Giessen area.

Then suddenly, the Fifth was ordered north to join III Corps in reducing the so-called Ruhr pocket. In this area the powerful German war materiel manufacturing was centered, for example, the famous Krupp weapons and munitions factories. Several crack German divisions were trapped in this heavily industrial area. So the war was not over after all. The 10th Combat Team was the first ordered to move out on April 7. And they were soon riding 100 miles anyway they could. Vehicle break downs meant they were short hundreds of men when it was time for their first attack.

737th Tank Battalion, Co. K, 2nd Infantry Regiment march through the newly taken town of Grevenstein en route to attack a nearby hill which the Germans are using as an observation post 11 April 1945. (US Army Photo)

The 1st Battalion was the first to attack on April 9, then the 2nd Battalion, and 3rd. Their mission was to check each village in their route of advance and subdue any resistance, and the next day the 1st Battalion had completed that task. Cleared villages included Beringhauser Klause, Meschede, Wallen, Siesse, Visbek, et. al.

By April 14, the 2nd Regiment was back in the thick of it too, and by the 16th, all zones were completely clear of resistance.

Then the problem became one of dealing with displaced persons, captured installations, and stray enemy troops in civilian dress—many of whom were trying to escape the area anyway they could. A recon platoon of the 737th Tank Battalion even scared up Lt. Gen. Kurt von Kortzfleisch, (second in command to Field Marshall Model). Corporal Frank Blick shot him in a gun fight at a hunting lodge near Schwammenberg.

This dramatic episode took place on April 20, the same day that our Division General Leroy "Red" Irwin was made the new XII Corps commander. He had been commander of the Fifth since June 2, 1943. An honor guard lined the streets of Menden as he bid his Red Diamond men farewell. Then on April 22, Maj. Gen. Albert E. Brown, a World War I veteran, took command of our division.

At any rate, the Fifth continued to do police and social service work in the Ruhr area—road blocks were set up, interrogations were held and so on. The 2nd and 11th Regiments processed literally thousands of prisoners as the Ruhr pocket collapsed. Slave laborers from other countries had been liberated and had to be cared for. Camps had to set up for them—many were starving and sick. Maj. John Hudspeth's camp at Menden is often cited as a model of efficiency and compassion. The Fifth was showing that no matter what their task, they were ready and willing.

Czechoslovakia

On April 25, our Fifth was ordered to rejoin the Third Army and the XII Corps, and ordered to move 300 miles southeast to Regen near the German-Austrian-Czech border. That took two days. Once there, the 10th Regiment immediately went to work with the mission of clearing a zone southeast along the Czech-German border. There was some light resistance, but the cold, rain and snow in the mountains made everything more difficult.

Then the Fifth was ordered on April 30 to attack again southeast in the direction of Linz and eliminate resistance. The plan was that the Third Army would press in from one side and the Russians from the other and crush the enemy in Czechoslovakia between.

By the end of April far north of here, the Russians had taken Berlin and our First Army was linking up with them. The Germans were putting up little organized defense any longer. The Wehrmacht's last stand in Czechoslovakia would be the Fifth Division's last assignment when many had already put down their arms.

Thankfully, resistance was light the first few days. Our 11th Regiment captured 200 Hungarians without a fight. Company I then took a bridge over the Muhle River. The towns of Ulrichsberg and Klaffer were cleared. There was sporadic fighting around Aigen. Many prisoners were pouring in. Hitler was reportedly dead, and Germans were giving up all over Europe, but here they had not received orders from Admiral Doenitz—Hitler's successor—to quit.

By May 4, the 1st and 2nd Battalions, 10th Inf. were driving deeper into the Sudentenland of Czechoslovakia, and crossing yet one more river—the Vltava in the Bohemian hills. While the 2nd Battalion forced a river crossing, the 3rd had seized Stozek and cleared a zone to the river.

The 1st Battalion captured Steinberg and Blochwald then Volary, and it was there the Americans saw first hand just what the enemy was made of. Jewish women from Poland and Hungary had been force-marched south from Poland, beaten constantly, and those who had given up dumped in common graves at Volary. As Gen. Eisenhower said later to Gen. Patton at the Buchenwald death camp, let as many of our men see this as possible to know for sure what we were fighting against. Around 60 of the Jewish survivors were liberated by our 2nd Combat Team and cared for by our Fifth Medical Battalion.

Division review in Czechoslovakia in May of 1945. (Courtesy of William Colon)

Enemy resistance was by now quelled in the 11th Regiment's zone and it was shifted north. A Fifth Infantry-4th Armored blow was planned by XII Corps at this time. The morning of May 6 found the Third Army driving on a 110 mile front deeper into Czechoslovakia. The 10th Regiment pushed eight more miles to Winterburg where the town's burgermeister came forward to meet Company F which was leading. This official surrendered to battalion commander Lt. Col. Harris Walker.

The Germans—the 1st SS Panzer Division—still refused at this time to talk peace, so once again the 2nd Battalion, 2nd Regiment, under Maj. Horace Townsend struck forward again. The 803 Tank Destroyer Battalion's recon platoon was in the lead on the morning of May 7 when they were ambushed. One Red Diamond man was killed and three wounded. After returning fire, the tank destroyers were withdrawing when a messenger from Maj. Pace raced up: "*Cease fire*," were his surprising words.

"*Cease fire and cease all forward movement*." This order had come to division headquarters at 0831.

Indeed, that morning at 0241 in France at Rheims, Col. Gen. Jodl had signed the unconditional surrender for the German army as our Lt. Gen. Walter Smith had also signed. The war was over. Let the sacrifice of that last Tank Destroyer soldier remind us what the Red Diamond men had been ready to give for ten long months in Europe since their jump off at Normandy. And let us say it again—the war was over. V-E Day—Victory in Europe Day—was celebrated on May 8 as millions rejoiced through the tears.

Here is how the 10th Regiment's historian characterizes their reaction: "*V-E Day was not the hilarious, rowdy occasion it might have been expected to be. The reaction of the men of the 10th was surprisingly cool and off-handed. Until now, daily existence had little complexity. 'Keep your powder dry, you stomach strong, and your fingers crossed' had been our simple but entirely practical philosophy. The newly won peace could not be reduced to a simple kill-or-be-killed practicability. Time hung heavily on our hands, and the first stunned shock of V-E Day held an air of unreality.*"

After The Shooting Stopped

However, after the German surrender, the Fifth Division's work was not about to be over. To begin with, the final link-up was in order, and Capt. Donald Robinson of the Fifth's Reconnaissance Troop made contact with the Russian 107th Infantry Division and established cordial relations.

Then there was the horrendous turmoil that the conquered nation was in. There was administration of the vast prisoner of war enclosures, the accounting of the enemy's equipment, the care and control of displaced persons and even the governing of the German civilians. Food, shelter, sanitation, and civil order were almost non-existent. To this end, the Fifth was ordered on May 21 to move north 80 miles to their Occupation Zone according to "Plan Eclipse."

This plan called for everything from the apprehension of war criminals to policing of black-market activities to the establishment of an entirely new economic system. In short, the Allies had a new country of their own to caretake one in ruins and chaos and full of grief, bitterness, hatred, and hopelessness—renegades, orphans, the raped, the starving, and the maimed.

The Fifth's territory was southeast Bavaria, and its division command post was set up in Vilshofen—some 80 miles northeast of Munich. Astride the Danube River, this occupation area covered roughly 1800 square miles and was bordered on the east and south by the German-Czech line.

Now our combat teams became control teams. Their first task was to round up and segregate the German military units in the area. The Czech border was closed and controlled. German prisoners numbering near 60,000 were returned to their rightful Russian captors who were only 30 miles away. Then the Red Diamond men took up the more mundane administrative tasks and settled into a garrison life which was far cry from what they had known for almost a year.

Part of 81mm Mortar Platoon, Co. M, 2nd Infantry at war's end in Volary, Czechoslovakia (l. to r.) Paige Fritz, Wilson Kirk, Leslie Langdeau, and Joe Rahie. (Courtesy of Joseph Rahie)

June 13, they turned the occupation area over to the 83rd Infantry Division, and on June 18 the first Fifth Division units left Vilshofen for the journey home. Home—had a word ever sounded so sweet?

Many would not come back. Some 667 enlisted men and 30 officers had been killed in action. Another 668 enlisted were missing in action along with 22 officers. Officers numbering 130 were listed as wounded in action—along with 3088 enlisted men. Together with non-battle casualties, the total number of division casualties came to 7,124.

The Fifth going home at war's end. FBI on banner refers to "Forgotten Bastards of Iceland," for the time the 5th Division spent there. (Courtesy of Joseph Rahie)

As the 10th Regiment's historian observes, the fighting record of the Fifth Division was brilliant. *"During the period of July 14 to May 8, 1944, we had been in almost constant contact with the enemy. The 10th alone had killed and wounded a staggering number of his men, captured 24,408 prisoners, and destroyed many of his best units. Against Wehrmacht, paratroopers, SS, or Volksturm we had never failed to take an objective. We had never failed to hold one. Caumont, Angers, Chartres, Montereau, Rheims, Verdun, Metz—there had been many more. We had assumed an almost amphibious status by establishing initial bridgeheads across the rivers Seine, Moselle, Seille, Sure, Sauer, Prum, Nims, Kyll, Rhine, and others."*

"Now it was over. Over for the living and the dead. However, we do not feel the team to have been broken by death. We—the 10th Regiment and all who fought with it—are still one."

Rail and motor columns took the men of the Fifth through Metz where 6,000 Americans lay in one cemetery alone. Then on to Rheims which you will remember the 2nd Combat Team had liberated—and where the German surrender had been signed. Tragically, in a train accident here one of the "old men" of the Fifth, Capt. Edward Martin of the 10th Regiment, was killed and many more injured. Capt. Martin had been on board since Iceland.

If that weren't unfortunate enough, on June 21, at the French Camp St. Louis, four men of Company G, 10th Regiment were killed and seven wounded by a dud high explosive 37mm. shell. Then early in July—while enroute to Camp Lucky Strike at Le Havre—a personnel carrier overturned killing four and injuring 14.

Sailing from Le Havre, the Fifth Division men began to arrive back in the states in late July and went immediately to separation centers where they were given a 30 day tour of duty at home for rest and recuperation. After this month's rehabilitation, they reassembled at Fort Campbell, Kentucky. The whole division had not assembled like this since their training days in England. By early September, the Division was reassembled and waiting for its next assignment to say "We Will."

As we close this chapter in the history of the Fifth Division let us glance back for a moment and look for a way to bring it to conclusion. The following excerpt from the 2nd Infantry Regimental history will speak for itself.

"Winter had set in on the Luxembourg front. Snow 12 inches deep covered the entire sector which the Regiment was to attack. The temperature had dropped to 16 degrees on the night of January 17-18 as the troops moved forward to assembly areas overlooking the Sauer River south of Ingeldorf."

"The crossing of the Sauer River was a surprise to the enemy—the newspapers said, but many a 2nd Infantry doughboy will dispute that statement. While the 1st Battalion made their crossings to the west of Ingeldorf, the 2nd Battalion—after bridging attempts failed east of town—marched down the river with every gun firing and literally blasted the enemy from his far shore defenses. But even after the assault boat crossing had been effected, the enemy continued to fight back from positions prepared on the high ground north of the river."

"Pvt. Charles H. Schroder, an automatic rifleman of Company F had been wounded in the crossing of the river, but like many another soldier that day, he refused evacuation in order to remain with his company. Lying exposed on the flat open ground between the Sauer River and the enemy positions on Goldknap Hill, he maintained a steady stream of fire at the enemy guns—which allowed his platoon to maneuver. Constantly exposed, he diverted enemy fire from his platoon until he was killed by artillery fire."

The heroism and sacrifice of men like Pvt. Schroder warranted many awards and citations for the Red Diamond men during World War II. These included 34 Distinguished Service Crosses, 602 Silver Stars, 2066 Bronze Stars, a large number of Purple Hearts, and Pvt. Harold Garman's Congressional Medal of Honor which we recounted earlier.

THE KOREAN WAR

The Fifth Division During The Korean Conflict

We saw in the previous section that as World War II drew to a close, the armies of the Soviet Union linked up with those of the Allies—for example, our Fifth Division joined with the Soviets against the Germans in Czechoslovakia. Then, after the war, just as our Fifth and other units occupied the defeated enemies' territories, so did the Soviet Union occupy much of Eastern Europe which it had liberated from Nazi regimes.

At the same time and in a similar fashion, the Soviets invaded the Korean peninsula in early August of 1945 after declaring war on the Japanese. Soon thereafter, the Japanese surrendered to the US, and thus began a prolonged occupation of Korea by the US and the Soviets. The Soviets saw to it that a communist regime was well entrenched in North Korea by 1948 when the United Nations called for free elections in both parts of the country. South Korea voted to be a democratic republic after the US withdrew, while the North refused to hold open elections after the Soviets withdrew. And hence, Korea became the divided country which would eventually be at war with itself.

The Korean War began on the morning of June 25, 1950 when the North Koreans crossed the border into the South all along the 38th parallel—and the fighting continued despite endless peace talks until July 27, 1953. In the end, 1.6 million Americans served in the Korean Theater of Operations; obviously then, an endless stream of troop replacements was needed, and the men of the Fifth Division—many of them skilled combat veterans—served as the trainers for many of those troops.

The Fifth Division had been reactivated as a training division at Fort Jackson, South Carolina on July 15, 1947. The philosophy behind this assignment made good sense: recruits trained by seasoned veterans with a legendary reputation would be more likely to develop fighting morale and esprit de corps. The men of the Fifth took more than 50,000 recruits through basic training there before it was inactivated in April of 1950, and so our division was ready to pick up there when the conflict in Korea heated up.

During the Korean War, the Fifth Infantry Division (Training) was reactivated at Indiantown Gap Military Reservation, Pennsylvania, on March 1, 1951, and by April 9 it was receiving its first inductees. Here are the main elements of this new Fifth: the 2nd, 10th, and 11th Infantry Regiments; Division Artillery—the 19th, 21st, 46th, and 50th Field Artillery Battalions, and the 47th Anti-Aircraft Artillery (Automatic Weapons) Battalion; 7th Engineer Battalion; 85th Tank Battalion, and the 5th Medical Battalion. The Division commanders included Col. Thomas J. Wells, Major General Lawrence B. Kaiser, and Major General George B. Barth.

The mission of this Fifth (Training) was "*...to receive, supply, train, and ship heavy and light Infantry replacements, and leadership students; to render administrative and logistical support to all Army, National Guard, and Air Force units stationed at the Military Reservation; and to rehabilitate the Military Reservation...*" To the end, it conducted branch immaterial or "basic training" (an eight week cycle) and infantry training (a sixteen week cycle). The basic leadership course conducted by the 7th Engineer Battalion for officer and enlisted cadre was eight weeks in length.

After sending many thousands of combat ready troops to Korea trained in the proud tradition of the Red Diamond, the Fifth (Training) was inactivated on September 1, 1953.

THE VIETNAM WAR

The Vietnam War

Our war in Vietnam was the longest in our history and perhaps the most controversial. Our involvement might be said to begin shortly after World War II just as our commitment in Korea had. In the period of the late 1940s and early 1950s, the Soviet annexation of the Eastern European countries, the communists' ascendance to power in China, the North Korea invasion of South Korean, and Vietnamese political leader Ho Chi Minh's ambitions for a united Vietnam were all seen by American political and military leaders as related parts of an international conspiracy.

This explains the American support in the late 1940s of the French-oriented Bao Dai government in South Vietnam. This policy was formalized in February 1950 when the US National Security Council concluded that a communist Indochina would more than likely lead to a communist Thailand and Burma. The council stated "*The balance of Southeast Asia would then be in grave hazard*," and what became known as the "Domino Theory" was born.

What logically followed from this theory was the policy that "*all practicable measures should be taken*" to stop a Viet Minh victory in the south, and thus our support of military aid to the French in their Vietnam colony as early as the Truman administration. Support for counter-insurgency in South Vietnam was in line with the Truman doctrine to contain the spread of communism world-wide. Use of American troops was debated this early and although decided against, by the time the French were lurching toward defeat at Dien Bien Phu, the US was funding 80% of the war effort there. And by that time, the Chinese Communists were generous supporters of the Viet Minh.

President Dwight D. Eisenhower was also convinced by the "Domino Theory" and the Truman Doctrine. Thus, after the fall of Dien Bien Phu to the Viet Minh in 1954, a long series of covert action began by the US Central Intelligence Agency. In addition, from as early as 1954 there were US military advisors in Vietnam. When Kennedy became President in 1960, he stepped up such action and continued other forms of aid. But the Pentagon could not deny that the leadership of the army of South Vietnam (ARVN) left much to be desired. The alternatives were to increase US military involvement—or get out altogether, and the Pentagon wanted in.

By 1960, the Viet Minh had formed the National Liberation Front (NFL) or Viet Cong (VC), and by that time their influence had spread to around 75% of the villages in the south. Its army was something like 20,000 strong, and in the early 1960s it was making runs on remote ARVN outposts. ARVN retaliation on suspected VC villages was sometimes careless and further polarized the peasants against the US supported Diem regime. In the eyes of many peasants, the Viet Cong were simply the lesser of the evils they had no choice but to accept.

What should President Kennedy do? Memories of Korea were still in the foreground, yet he chose not to abandon our South Vietnam allies; he chose not to allow a communist victory which could only encourage such aggression elsewhere, yet he died before he had fully committed the US beyond the point of no return.

When Kennedy took office, the number of our military advisors in Vietnam was around 900—that's not counting large numbers of CIA. By the time of the President's assassination there was upwards of

11,000. When his Vice President Lyndon Johnson took over, we were poised at the threshold of deeper military involvement. And although President Johnson too did not want to commit the US to a full-fledged war, the administration he inherited was already largely pro-war, and his gradual escalation of the conflict over the next few years amounted to the same thing.

In August of 1964, he asked Congress for the power to do what was necessary to defend our forces already in South Vietnam, and our countries longest war was underway with the Gulf of Tonkin Resolution. To complicate our mission, the President saw the defeat of the Hanoi regime in the north as essential. The north had its army (the NVA) in addition to the Viet Cong in the south.

Stepped up VC attacks in 1964-65 caused US casualties and led Johnson and his military leaders to begin Operation Rolling Thunder—a campaign of air strikes on the north. And by March 8, two battalions of American Marines were wading ashore to defend our largest air base at Da Nang. Our troop strength was by then 27,000—and by October, it was 148,000. The leaders in Hanoi had miscalculated when they concluded the US would never enter into a land war in Southeast Asia. By August of 1967, there were over half a million American soldiers in Vietnam.

The Fifth Division In Vietnam

By June 1968, our 1st Infantry Brigade, Fifth Infantry Division (Mech) was in South Vietnam where it would serve until August of 1971. While there, it would play an important role in eleven important combat operations beginning with "Massachusetts Bay" (April 23 to June 15, 1969) through "Montana Mustang" (April 8 to April 13, 1971).

Our 1st Brigade (Mech) was alerted for deployment to Vietnam on March 25, 1968. It then underwent a 13 week training program with emphasis on independent small unit tactics and rapid response to alerts. It had been greatly changed from the outfit we brought home from Europe after World War II; it was modified and supplemented to meet new needs in a very different kind of war. At its peak, it had over 6,000 personnel, and its many diverse elements—including five battalions—were as follows:

Headquarters and Headquarters Company, of course, then, 1st Battalion, 11th Infantry; 1st Battalion, 61st Infantry (Mech); 1st Battalion, 77th Armor; "A" Troop, 4th Squadron, 12th Cavalry; 5th Battalion, 4th Artillery; 75th Support Battalion; "A" Company, 7th Engineers; and 517th Military Intelligence Detachment.

The highly specialized nature of this modern army is evident in some of the other units added to the 1st Brigade during the war:

3rd Squadron, 5th Cavalry; 298th Signal Company; "P" Company (Ranger), 75th Infantry; "D" Troop, 5th

SSG. James A. Smith, 1st Signal Brigade, 5th Mech Division one of many students from various units to be taught the operation of the ANGRC-163 radio 16 September 1968. (National Archives US Army Photo)

Cavalry (Air Mobile); 407th Radio Research Detachment; 86th Chemical Detachment; 48th Public Information Detachment; 77th Combat Engineer Battalion; and 43rd Scout Dog Platoon.

Now, in its legendary Tet Offensive, Gen. Giap's Viet Cong and North Vietnamese Army risked everything on an all out attack across the board in January 1968—from the Marine's fire base at Khe Sanh to most of the South's major cities and provincial capitals. Giap's plan was that the fight at Khe Sanh would distract the US and ARVN troops while the other attacks were launched, and the US and friends would find themselves spread too thin to win anywhere.

Battles raged throughout January and February, and by the middle of February it was clear Giap's attacks were flagging thanks to fierce US/ARVN resistance and air power. The southern cities did not fall, neither did Khe Sanh. Giap had lost 45,000 men and 7,000 had been taken prisoner, but he had proved that his army was no where near defeated, and many more American troops were needed if that were ever to be. Casualties on our side totaled over 20,000. And although Johnson asked for more troops in the wake of Tet, his most important advisors and the CIA director as well were now pessimistic about a victory in this most unconventional war. A turning point in the overall shape of the war had been reached.

A Chaplain conducts a service during the combined U.S. Army, Marine, and ARVN Operation "Utah Mesa" in July of 1969. (National Archives US Army Photo)

The enemy losses during Tet showed how determined and willing to sacrifice he was. And it was into such a grave situation that—by July 22, 1968—our 1st Brigade had completely arrived in Vietnam at Quang Tri base. (Three maneuver battalions were located at outlying base camps).

Quang Tri City was a provincial capital on the east coast in the far north of South Vietnam, not far from the Demilitarized Zone along which heavy fighting took place. In addition to the Brigade's own operations, its Quang Tri base was also near enough to the Marine fire base at Khe Sanh to offer it support—to help turn its units into more mobile strike forces with our armored personnel carriers, and with our tanks to supply the Marines with the shock power they needed. Moreover, at Quang Tri, the Brigade was near enough to aid in interfering with traffic on the Ho Chi Minh where enemy troops and supply moved.

From Quang Tri west to the Laotian border the terrain ranged from gently rolling plateau to high, steep mountains. The plateau might be covered with elephant grass 15 feet tall. The plateau might be heavily eroded, and the mountains might be covered with dense undergrowth and cut with numerous mountain streams—all conditions which needless to say are not at all suited for tracked vehicles. In addition, the weather was often characterized by low visibility with low clouds and fog into mid-morning which made air supply difficult. Temperatures from the mid-90s to 105 were common.

The 1st Brigade had joined the fight in the bloodiest year of the war, and according to its orders, its mission was "*to conduct pacification, strike, counter-infiltration and counter-insurgency operations throughout the populated areas of Quang Tri Province and in Base Area 101.*" This involved conducting

Two M-113 armored personnel carriers from Troop "A", 4th Squadron, 12th Cavalry sweep an area for the enemy 10 June 1969. (National Archives US Army Photo)

A tracked fuel vehicle from the 1st Brigade is re-supplied during Operation "Utah Mesa" in the Ashau Valley in July of 1969. (National Archives US Army Photo)

Gun crew awaits firing orders 30 October 1970. (National Archives US Army Photo)

Members of Co. "A", 1st Battalion, 61st Infantry move out on patrol along the DMZ 23 August 1970. (National Archives US Army Photo)

"*small unit (squad and fire team) search and clear operations, combined operations with ARVN and Provincial forces, "Hunter-Killer" operations, and saturation ambushes and patrols at night.*" The emphasis was "*on cutting the enemy's lines of communications between the old base areas in the mountains and the population in the lowlands, as well as interdicting his movement within the populated areas.*" To this end, Brigade forces often ambushed between their base area and the population centers. These ambushing and patrolling missions had the added benefit of revealing any large enemy entrance to the area.

The first Brigade unit to be tactically committed was Company "A," 1st Battalion, 77th Armor. It was moved north of Con Thien August 12, 1968 to support the 1st Marine Regiment against the NVA units which were infiltrating the DMZ. In ten successful days, Company "A" made five enemy contacts and was credited with 80 enemy kills. And with this, a fierce fighting tradition began for the Fifth Division in Vietnam.

The 1st Brigade moved into the area called "Leatherneck Square" on August 26, and its first operations in force took place there. According to the Fifth's Vietnam historian, "*Elements of the 11th Infantry and 77th Armor overran a bunker complex where 52 NVA were killed. Throughout the next two months, the First conducted battalion-size operations in and around the DMZ effectively utilizing the fire power and mobility of tanks and armored personnel carriers.*"

A soldier of the 1st Battalion, 11th Infantry watches his footing while on patrol in the jungles southwest of Quang Tri. (Northernmost Publication Photo courtesy of Harry Scott)

Between October 23 and 26, 1st Battalion, 61st Infantry, and Company B, 77th Armor swept into the DMZ itself. A fierce battle ensued. At first, the infantry was pinned down with heavy mortar and machine gun fire. Then "*the tanks were committed in a cavalry-like charge on the flank of the battle and routed the NVA into the open...inflicting heavy casualties upon them.*" In four days of fighting, 303 enemy were killed, and 258 individual and 16 crew-served weapons were taken. Such weapon seizure was extraordinary and indicated the severity of the rout.

In the months which followed, the Brigade's task organization was changed often as the situation warranted. Typical of First Brigade activity was a series of operations in the 3rd Marine area of operations where it fought major battles along the DMZ and around Con Thien such as the Battle of Cam Hung. A series of operations was also conducted on the Khe Sanh Plains by an Armor/Tech Task Force.

Sp.4 Lacy Davis, Jr., point man for the 3rd Squad, 2nd Platoon, Co. C, 1st Battalion, 61st Infantry Regiment, recalls a battle near Khe Sanh not far from the Ho Chi Minh Trail, Camp LZ Saigon. He does not date it, but his description gives us a sense of what the battle described above was like in detail.

Sp.4 Davis' squad was with HHQ Company which included about 50 men and two tanks. Their perimeter, he reports, "*was so narrow you could pitch a stone across it*," when it was completely surrounded the NVA. "*I knew if we were hit, we would be overrun*." So, they dug in. He had plenty of grenades on hand—the kind without muzzle flash for night fighting, his M-16, and a loaded .45 in each front pocket.

"*Then (around 3:00 a.m.) the whole world exploded*." The NVA attacked. "*More RPGs were coming at us than mosquitoes in the air. It lasted until sun up*." (Here, he skips ahead, and leaves the actual battle to our imaginations).

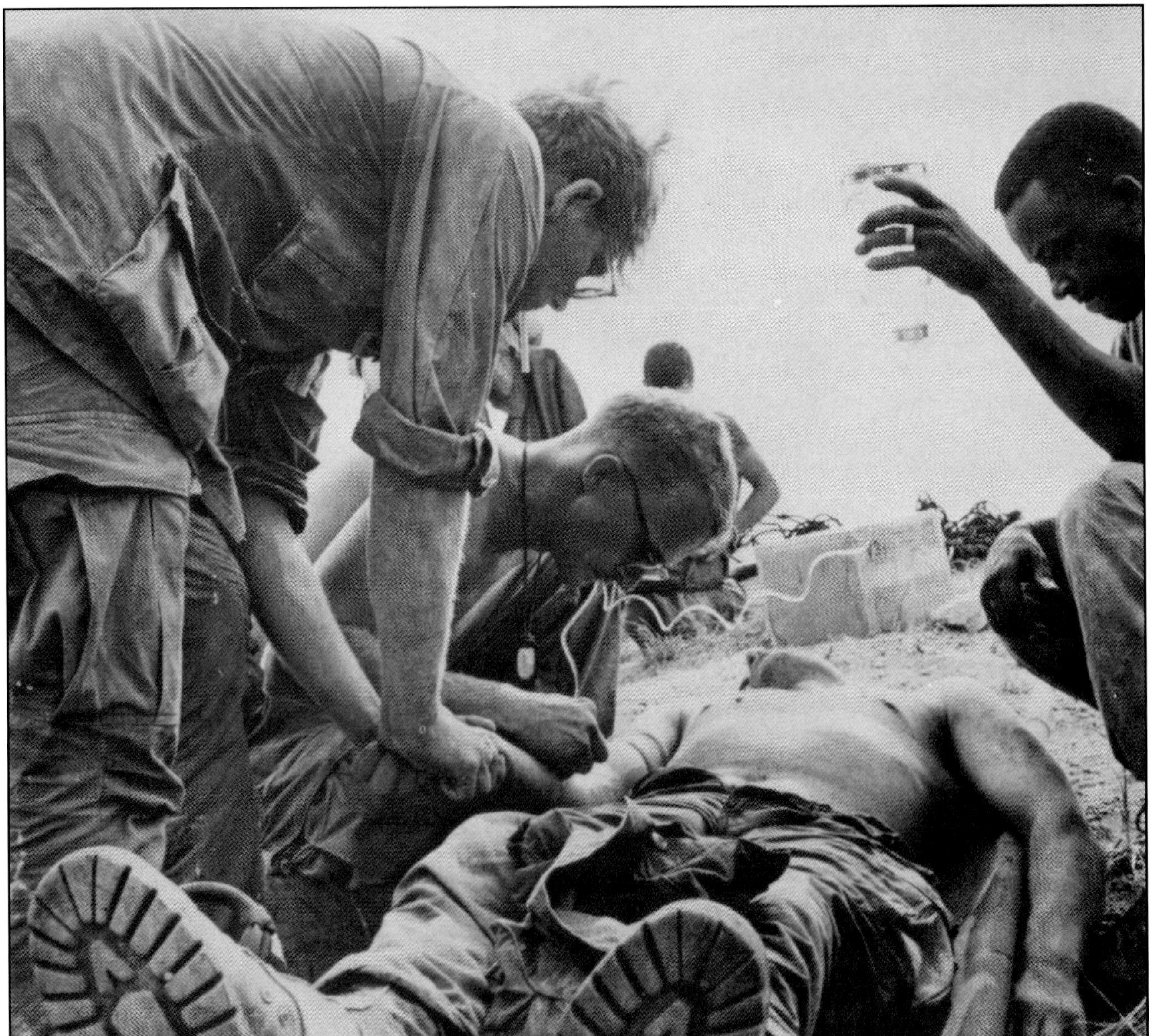

Fighting to save a life, medics of the 1st Battalion, 11th Infantry aid a wounded soldier during an operation about three miles south of the DMZ. (Northernmost Publication Photo courtesy of Harry Scott)

"I got out of my foxhole and walked over to my black buddy Burton's hole. He was wounded, and his hands were burnt bad from changing red hot barrels in his M.60 machine gun. I gave him help out of his foxhole. Lt. Rich said, 'Burton, a chopper is coming in, and you need to leave the field. I'll put you in for a Silver Star, and thanks for hanging in there.'"

"The rest of the Squad had already been medevaced. I never remembered what happened to any of my Squad except Burton from North Carolina. They were all gone, but we lost very few. And there was NVA people lying everywhere from a few feet of our perimeter to about 150 meters down into the woods. We stacked them up like cord wood. I would say we were hit by 400, because they left behind about 150 KIA, and when possible they carried their dead and wounded. We killed a few Chinese in that battle too."

During Tet in January and February of 1969, Brigade operations (ambushing and patrolling) were successful to the extent that captured enemy documents indicated he felt he could no longer enter the populated portions of Trieu Phong, Hai Lang, and Mai Linh. By the end of February, our First had conducted more than 37 such operations, and the enemy had not even been able to attack us or any friendly forces or installations. The Brigade also provided transportation for refugees, construction materials, and established medical aid visits to friendly villages.

The danger during patrol operations is well illustrated by another of Sp.4 Lacy Davis's personal reports. His 11 man squad of Charlie Company, 1st Battalion, 61st Infantry, was moving south toward Con Thien when their spotter plane identified about 200 NVA west of them. This was near noon. Then, minutes later, about 150 more were spotted to the east. "*Forget about the booby traps,*" Lt. James Slocket ordered, "*let's get the hell out of here.*"

To top it off, then, the plane radioed again with 75 NVA spotted directly in front of the little squad. After calculating their chance of survival, Sp. Davis thought, "*My God, we're dead. No chance in hell. This is it, just let me know I killed the S.O.B. that killed me.*"

A-4 Fire Support Base

Tracking through a field near A-4 & C-2.

Soldiers at A-4 waiting for a chopper.

(Photos courtesy of Harry Scott)

Fire Mission! "Shot, Over"

Two gun pits at A-4

A gunner cleaning his gun poses for the camera.

(Photos courtesy of Harry Scott)

"We played the cat and mouse game til dark. At times, the NVA was so close we could hear them on each side. Lt. Slocket and the spotter used beeping signals to let us know when to take a step to the west or to the east until the plane was low on gas and had to leave. At dark we paired off, got back to back, and sat straight down in place. From time to time I thought I can't take it anymore. I kept thinking I hope nobody cracks and starts shooting."

"We sat in place til about 9:00 the next morning—and the spotter plane came back looking for our bodies. The pilot couldn't believe it when he said "23, over," and Lt. Slocket said, "23, go ahead."

Sp. Davis was later awarded the Bronze Star and Purple Heart for his heroism in a Brigade operation (involving tanks and armored personnel carriers) in which his unit was ambushed, and his 3rd Squad largely decimated. Stories such as his are told, of course, by survivors—but at what price? Mr. Davis is even today suffering from Post Traumatic Stress Syndrome.

In late February, the 3rd Squadron, 5th Cavalry (which was newly assigned to the Fifth Division) made contact for two days with the enemy west of Quang Tri. They were aided by eight battalions of artillery, and the 16 inch gun of the battleship New Jersey bombarded the enemy. 1st Brigade casualties were three killed and 35 wounded.

In the local elections of March 1969, the Brigade helped insure that the Provincial Forces would be able to secure the voters. Also during this month and April, our Brigade continued to give strong support to the troops in the "Leatherneck Square" area and at Khe Sanh. "Rice Denial Operations" cut the enemy's supply lines and searched out enemy rice supplies.

In April and May, 1969, the famous Fifth Division 7th Engineers opened a road to give the 3rd Marines a route from Quang Tri to Vandergrift Combat Base. The engineers often had to clear the roads of mines and obstacles.

April 25, the Ranger Team of "P" Company, 75th Infantry ambushed and killed Eguyen Quyet, a major guerilla leader in the province, a communist security chief, and a terror and assassination cadre commander. Such a list of duties indicates how dirty and brutal a war our First Brigade was immersed in.

In June, elements of the 1st Battalion, 61st Infantry and 1st Battalion, 77th Armor combined with Marines in the Khe Sanh area for operations against the NVAs 24th Regiment. The enemy body count totaled 147 with only light First casualties. This nine day engagement brought home the value of armored vehicles even when the terrain is not suitable for them. These same two First battalions remained with the Marines throughout July providing them with a mobile strike force and shock power of tanks and the other armored they needed.

Members of the 1st Battalion, 77th Armor stand guard atop their armored personnel carrier during a break in operations near Cua Viet. (Northernmost Publication Photo courtesy of Harry Scott)

In August, the Brigade was still serving all needs in the "Leatherneck Square" area, but then on October 22, it was removed from the 3rd Marine Division operational control and placed under the commanding general of XXIV Corps. With the 1st ARVN, the Brigade was now completely responsible for defending Quang Tri and Dan Ho combat base.

The same ambush and patrol activities continued, and these led to contact with the NVA 27th Regiment from 11-18 November on the part of the hard fighting 1st Battalion, 61st Infantry as well as two companies of 1st Battalion, 77th Armor. Two days later, the enemy was in retreat west toward the Laotian border. Private Stanley Samulak, Company C, 1st Battalion, 61st Infantry, was awarded the Army Commendation Medal with "V" Device for his heroism in this fight.

According to his award citation, Pvt. Samulak distinguished himself "*while on a sweep and clear operation...on 12 November 1969. While maneuvering through enemy occupied terrain near Cam Lo, an unknown element from the 27th NVA Regiment opened fire on the point element of the 1st Platoon wounding the point man and the aidman. Disregarding their personal safety, Pvt. Samulak and two comrades maneuvered through the intense fire and retrieved the two injured men and removed them to the safety of a covered position. His selfless courage undoubtedly saved the lives of the two men.*"

Specially trained dogs are used effectively by the Division to track enemy personnel and to detect mines. (Northernmost Publication Photo courtesy of Harry Scott)

Troops from the 1st Battalion, 61st Infantry prepare to leave a defensive position as the 1st Battalion, 77th Armor stands guard during an operation west of Charlie 2. (Northernmost Publication Photo courtesy of Harry Scott)

RIF (reconnaissance in force) patrol of 1st Battalion, 11th Infantry returns to Eagle Support Base C-2 near DMZ after days operation. (National Archives US Army Photo)

A self-propelled 155mm Howitzer of the 5th Battalion, 4 Artillery, which was part of the fire support for Operation "Dewey Canyon II". (National Archives US Army Photo)

That same day, Pvt. Samulak was wounded in combat by a enemy RPG. He reports that "*we were outnumbered by at least 3 to 1. I laid in the field 18 hours before being rescued.*" He received the Purple Heart and Combat Infantry Badge in addition to his Commendation Medal.

In the first few months of 1970, the Brigade provided security for the South Vietnamese village pacification program. Then things heated up as the 1st of the 61st again engaged the enemy for three fierce days of fighting—sometimes hand to hand. Sixty NVA troops were killed, a command post was overrun, and much enemy equipment captured.

To push ahead, the Brigade was reinforced in late 1970 and in January 1971, Operation Lam Son 719 was begun under Brig. Gen. John C. Hill. The 1st Brigade both constructed and was charged with securing the QL9 road from Dong Ha to the Laotian border—as well as access roads to Khe Sanh. It was along this route that a 20,000 troop ARVN Task Force moved toward Laos. In addition, the Brigade was ordered to provide mobile defense for the huge forward support area of Vandergrift and Khe Sanh.

This from the Brigade history sums up the Operation Lam Son action: "*For 69 days of increasingly confused and bitter fighting, the Brigade prevented the enemy from making a successful offensive move against any of these vital links in the ARVN offensive. A body count of 400 North Vietnamese was made, and the primary mission to keep the logistical support channels fully operational at all times was accomplished.*"

From April 8 to April 30, the Brigade participated in combat operation Montana Mustang. Then, in June, it "*received its stand-down orders with stateside deployment to commence on July 1.*"

During 1969, President Nixon had ordered troop cutbacks of over 100,000, and they were continuing in 1970. In addition, General Westmoreland had been replaced by Gen Creighton Abrams whose mission was the "Vietnamization" of the war. Frontline ARVN units were given a wide variety of artillery and armor. The idea of "Vietnamization" was not new, but in 1969 and 70, the scale of military aid was increased as it was made clear that US troops would be steadily pulled out. Saigon had no choice but to take more and more responsibility for the war.

Delta Company, 75th Support Battalion returns from operations at Khe Sanh. (Northernmost Publication Photo courtesy of Harry Scott)

In mid-1971, Brigade Commander Brigadier General Harold Dunwoody limited the First Brigade's activity to "*base security in anticipation of a NVA effort to achieve a propaganda victory over the departing unit. The Brigade colors departed Quang Tri on 8 August 1971,*" after a ceremony in which Vietnamese decorations were awarded to Brigade personnel.

"*The Brigade returned to Fort Carson, leaving the defense of Quang Tri in the hands of the ARVN 1st Division, a unit it had largely trained. Then on 22 August 1971, the Brigade colors were inactivated at Fort Carson....*" A powerful force for the United States in Vietnam was finally at rest.

Looking back, we see that not long after Tet 1968, President Johnson announced the cessation of bombing in the North and his willingness to negotiate a settlement with Hanoi, and last but not least—owing in part to the growing opposition at home, he announced he would not run again for President in 1968. President Nixon had run for office and won on a pledge to pull us out of Vietnam with honor. Nevertheless, the peace negotiations in Paris and the brutal battles in Vietnam continued another five years after that turning point in 1968. And it would not be until April 30, 1975, that the North Vietnamese Army tanks rolled into Saigon, and the 30 year war for the Vietnamese was finally over.

In summary, the American military was never defeated in Vietnam; in fact, it won every major engagement in which it participated. Yet it was a war we can not say we won or lost in the sense in which the Allies won World War II. We chose to withdraw rather than fight to a clearly defined end, if indeed, a real military victory was possible in this kind of war. It is quite possible that any military solution to the political problems of the Vietnamese was impossible.

One thing we are certain of, however, is that the 1st Brigade, 5th Infantry Division (Mech) fought with valor and distinction as had its predecessors. Perhaps Sp. 4 Lacy Davis from Merrell Mountain, Alabama sums it up well for the men of the fighting Fifth: "*We were the Bloody Red Devils. I walked point on DMZ from the Ho Chi Minh Trail to the South China Sea. We patrolled the DMZ setting ambushes and being ambushed, living in foxholes. Battles were many, rest was little.*"

A soldier from the P 75th Ranger Company moves slowly through elephant grass during a reconnaissance mission. (Northernmost Publication Photo courtesy of Harry Scott)

After reactivation in 1975, and down through the late 1970s and 1980s, the Fifth Division participated in training and exercises of many types. The well-known REFORGER—or Return of Forces to Germany—was an annual exercise typical of the Red Diamond men—or the Red Devils, as the Vietnam GI's called themselves. REFORGER was conducted under the auspices of the Supreme Allied Commander, Europe, and took the Fifth back to a German which was now an ally, thanks to their sacrifice.

This REFORGER exercise involved deployment of forces and equipment to the Federal Republic of Germany, participation in NATO field training exercises, and redeployment of forces back to the US. In REFORGER 1978, a typical year, the Fifth Division was tasked with planning and executing the movement of all CONUS-based forces to Germany—that was over 13,000 troops with 6,115 from the Fifth itself.

And so it went for the Fifth Division during the rest of the Cold War years. Their ever-ready spirit and their contribution to an ever-vigilant NATO force helped wear the empire of the Soviet Union down to final dissolution.

PANAMA

Operation "Just Cause"

After months of deteriorating relations the governments of the United States and that of dictator Manuel Noriega of Panama, the situation became critical with the killing of a Marine officer and the harassment of American personnel by the Noriega forces. When it came time for President Bush to call a halt to Noriega's repressive regime, the Red Diamond was standing in the wings and ready to be called. A part of the division had been deployed in the Panama City area in May 1989 to secure American facilities

The following September these troops were replaced by "Task Force Regulars", named for the sobriquet of the 6th Infantry Regiment earned at the Battle of Chippewa in 1814. This task force consisted of the 4th Battalion, 6th Infantry, 5th Division (Mechanized) with supporting elements and was assigned the mission of the assault of "La Comandancia", headquarters of Noriega's Panama Defense Forces (PDF). Augmenting the 4th Battalion, 6th Infantry were Co. A, 7th Engineers, elements of the 5th Battalion, 1st Field Artillery, 5th Support Battalion (Forward), Co. C, 508th Airborne Infantry Regiment, four M551 Sheridans from the 82nd Airborne Division, four Marine light armored vehicles (LAVs) and two platoons of military police from Fort Benning Georgia.

The invasion of Panama opened in the first hours of December 20, 1989 when Task Force Regulars, briefed on their mission the previous evening, moved into position shortly after midnight to establish road blocks north and south of La Comandancia. Companies B and D and a platoon of Co. C, 6th Infantry led the assault with the Airborne company and the engineers following. The Sheridans and the Marine LAVs set up fire support positions to help isolate La Comandancia. Close air support was provided by the Air Force's AC 130 Spectre fire support aircraft.

An estimated 300–400 PDF troops defended the 15 building compound of La Comandancia and fought fiercely to defend their positions against the advancing American task force. Heavy fighting continued for the next three hours. Heavy fighting was also taking place in other parts of the city.

Company A, 4th Battalion, 6th Infantry was attached to the 5th Battalion, 87th Infantry Regiment and this force became involved in heavy fighting to seize key positions around Panama City. A mechanized platoon with supporting Sheridans and Marine LAVs were later sent to provide security for the American Embassy.

By dawn of the 20th, all the task force objectives were secured. The heavy fighting was over but some sniping continued. At 11:00 a.m. a Ranger company was added and the task force began clearing the Comandancia and remaining buildings in the compoound and had them secured by 5:00 p.m. Some sporadic fighting continued for the next several days as Task Force Regulars performed security missions n the area. The task force's mission "Operation Just Cause," came to an end with the loss of personnel of two Regulars killed in action, one each, in companies A and B, and 34 wounded. With the successful completion of the division"s mission the President's objectives had been met and Manuel Noriega was taken into custody and returned to face charges in an American court.

Task Force Regulars returned to Fort Polk in late January. The returned veterans of the Panama engagement were honored with a division review on February 9 with awards being made at the ceremony. Another chapter was added to the long and distinguished history of one of the finest division in the U.S. Army: The Fighting Fifth!

A major player in the hottest combat or the most complex peacetime exercises, the Fifth Infantry Division was last inactivated November 24, 1992, at Fort Polk, Louisiana—the end of a distinguished history of service and sacrifice. By a fateful coincidence, the inactivation took place 75 years to the day after the order was issued to activate the new Fifth Infantry Division on November 24, 1917.

References

Baldwin, Hanson. Battles Lost and Won. Harpers, New York, 1948.

Beckett, Brian. The Illustrated History of the Vietnam War. Gallery Book, New York, 1985.

Berry, Henry. Make the Kaiser Dance. Doubleday, New York, 1978.

Davidson, Lt. Gen. Phillip. Vietnam at War. Presidio Press, Novato, California, 1988.

Farago, Ladislas. Patton: Ordeal and Triumph. Oblensky, New York, 1964.

The Fifth Infantry Division in the ETO. Fifth Division Historical Section, HQ, Fifth Inf. Div. Albert Love Enterprises, 1945. *Including Photographs.*

History of the 11th Infantry Regiment. PR Section, HQ, 11th Inf. Reg.

History of the 2nd Infantry Regiment. PR Section, HQ, 2nd Inf. Reg.

History of the 10th Infantry Regiment. PR Section, HQ, 10th Inf. Reg.

Lynch, John L., Capt. All of It I Knew, Some of It I Saw, Part of It I Was. Lynch, Phoenix, Arizona, 1989.

Marshall, S. L. A. Brig. Gen., Ret. The American Heritage History of WWI. American Heritage Pub., New York, 1964.

Perret, Geoffrey. There's a War to be Won: US Army in WWII. Random House, New York, 1991.

Pimlott, John. Vietnam: The History and the Tactics. Crescent, New York, 1982.

Spector, Ronald. After Tet: The Bloodiest Year In Vietnam. Macmillan, New York, 1993.

Stallings, Lawrence. The Doughboys. Harper & Row, New York, 1963.

Weintraub, Stanley. A Stillness Heard Round The World. Dutton, New York, 1985.

U S ARMY
9B 1258

VETERANS OF THE FIFTH INFANTRY DIVISION

Members of the 1st Battalion, 5th Mech Division rest atop an M-48 tank during Operation "Fisher" 6 January 1969. (National Archives US Army Photo)

CASPER J. ALAGNA, was born Aug. 11, 1921 in Brooklyn and enlisted September 1940. He trained at Camp Custer, MI; went to Iceland in September 1941 with HQ Co., 1st Bn., 10th Inf. Div. He learned the Morse Code and joined the communication platoon. He soon made staff sergeant and took over the platoon.

Landing in France on June 6+5, he was soon in the Battle of the Bulge where he was awarded the Purple Heart and the Bronze Star with three Battle Stars.

In July 1945 he was discharged at Fort Sheridan, IL. He married Nancy Martinico on July 28, 1946. They have four married sons and five grandchildren. He worked for the railroad and then the airlines from where he retired.

He and his wife do a lot of travelling

FRANK ALBANESE (BUDDY), was born Aug. 5, 1921 in Williamson, WV. He enlisted in the Army on Nov. 4, 1940 and was inducted at Fort Thomas, KY. He served with Co. E, 10th Inf. at Fort Thomas and while in training at Fort Custer, MI.

Transferred to Co. A, 10th Inf. in August 1941 for the duration. Went overseas to Iceland in September 1941 and assigned as company bugler. Landed in Normandy on July 9, 1944, assigned to 3rd Plt. as an assistant squad leader and fought in Normandy, Northern France, Rhineland, Ardennes and Central Europe. He was wounded twice.

Memorable experience: "On March 26, 1945, during the capture of Frankfurt and while the town was still being secured, Co. A received orders at dusk to hold and secure positions. I was assigned to lead a patrol in the general vicinity of our immediate front.

"During this assignment we came upon a German cement bunker and for precaution, I ordered the patrol detail to take cover and remain outside the bunker while I checked inside. The bunker was deep and the cement steps were very dark leading downward into a small opening. When I finally reached the entrance, it was so dark that I had to take my GI L-shaped flashlight from my belt. Buddy threw a beam of light around and saw a few Germans, one with a burp gun pointed directly at me. I thought sure that he was going to shoot, but he didn't. Instead he hollered 'Comrade' and immediately surrendered along with the rest. What a tremendous relief, as I was so damn scared my heart seemed to drop down to my shoes. The next thing I knew this older German sergeant, who spoke a little English, began telling me how he hated Hitler (so he said). Our orders were to secure and defend our positions, so we decided to remain in the bunker for the rest of the night—besides it had gotten pitch dark outside.

"One of the Germans produced some dice, a kerosene lamp was found and ignited, a tarpaulin was miraculously produced to cover the entrance and the crap game began. The Germans cleaned up, winning all of the money. The next morning at daylight, before the prisoners were sent back to the Company CP, one of our men was a very big loser and, of course, wanted his money back and relieved the Germans of it before they left. They even laughed about the whole thing, later this GI excused himself by rationalizing that prisoners can't use money."

Highest rank achieved was staff sergeant. He was discharged on June 19, 1945 compiling 137 points. He is now retired after 35 years of service with the General Electric Company.

GEORGE W. BACHMAN, was born Jan. 16, 1919 in Williamston, MI. He was in the first draft from Ingham County and was inducted Jan. 28, 1941 at Fort Custer. Was assigned to C Btry., 21st FA Bn. and trained at Fort Custer, Fort McCoy, Iceland (1942), England (1943), Ireland (1943). Landed at Utah Beach July 10, 1944.

When the war ended, he was in Czechoslovakia. He earned five Battle Stars and the Bronze Star. He held the rank of T/5 forward observer and was discharged from Fort Sheridan in July 1945.

In 1946 he enlisted in the Michigan National Guard, was commissioned as second lieutenant in 1950 and retired in 1969 with the rank of major, assistant G3, 46th Inf. Div. He transferred to 5033 USAR School, retiring as LTC in 1972 with 30 years service.

Worked 29 years for General Motors Olds Div., retiring in 1981. He married Norma Sober in 1950 and has a son and granddaughter. His leisure time is spent collecting and reading military history. Has been in the Orient and Europe five times. He is Past National President Society 5th Inf. Div.

CHESTER E. BALL (CHET), was born Aug. 19, 1921 in Seth, WV. Was drafted July 4, 1942 and assigned to 314th FA, 80th Div., July 25, 1942, at Camp Forrest, TN. Was promoted to corporal August 1942; Field Artillery OCS November 1942; commissioned second lieutenant Jan. 28, 1943; joined 590th FA, 106th Div., Ft. Jackson, SC, Feb. 15, 1943; promoted to first lieutenant August 1943.

He volunteered for overseas September 1943, joined 5th Div. at Tidworth, England, October 1943. He moved to Northern Ireland November 1943; landed at Utah Beach, Normandy, D-plus 28, 1944. Battery Executive, C Btry., 50th FA; forward observer with C Btry. Transferred to 46th FA December 1944 as forward observer.

Assigned as liaison officer, 46th FA in April 1945. Observed General Patton urinating in Rhine River on morning of March 23, 1945 from east bank of the river. On approach to Frankfurt, Germany, met a rifleman who showed him a "souvenir" he had taken from a German soldier. It was a map of the AA defenses of Frankfurt with all positions and command posts pin-point plotted. He confiscated the "souvenir" and the rifleman was "mad as hell." The map was sent to Corp and Army artillery for firing on the positions during the night before we reached Frankfurt.

Battles and campaigns for Battle Stars: Normandy, Northern France, Ardennes, Rhineland, and Central Europe. His decorations include the Silver Star, Bronze Star with one cluster and V (valor) device, Purple Heart with two Oak Leaf Clusters, World War II European Theater Medal with five Battle Stars, American Theater Medal, World War II Army of Occupation Medal (Europe), World War II Victory Medal, and the Army Reserve Ribbon with two Hour Glass devices (for more than 30 years service).

After returning home in July 1945, developed infection in leg wound and was asked to report to hospital at Ft. Meade, MD but declined so he could take command of troop train to Camp Campbell, KY. At Campbell he received promotion orders (dated July 1, 1945) to captain. Reported to hospital at Campbell on August 25 where he met two second lieutenant Army nurses and married one of them, Lt. Betty Hively, on Dec. 29, 1945. Betty passed away at Cambridge, OH on July 25, 1992. They had three children: Beth Elaine Watkins, Harry Stuart and Chester E. Jr.

Was valedictorian of high school class in May 1938. Received bachelor degree in journalism at Marshall College, Huntington, WV (1942). Upon separation and commissioned in Army Reserve in 1945, attended Ohio State University and received master's degree in journalism and taught at Marshall. Joined Ohio State Journalism faculty in 1951. After five years was appointed editor and reprographics director in the College of Engineering for seven years. Appointed to similar position in the OSU Research Foundation in 1963. Retired from OSU as Emeritus Assistant Professor, Photography and Cinema in March 1981.

Life member of 5th, 80th, and 106th Div. associations; DAV; Military Order of the Purple Heart; Reserve Officers Association; Marshall and OSU Alumni associations; OSU Faculty Club, OSU Retirees Association, and In-Plant Management Association. Member of Hilliard (Ohio) American Legion.

Elected to four terms on Hilliard Board of Education and three terms on Hilliard Charter Commission. Member and past president of Hilliard Kiwanis, American Field Services, Epilepsy Association of Central Ohio, and citizens associations.

Eagle Scout 1935, editor of high school and college student papers, played trumpet in high school and college marching bands.

Retired in 1981 from OSU and Army Reserve as colonel, deputy information officer of 1st U.S. Army. Currently owner of Sir Speedy Printing Center in Columbus, OH.

MILTON F. BARTELT, was born in Cleveland, OH in 1922. He enlisted Feb. 5, 1942; went to basic training at Ft. McClellen, AL and joined L Co., 10th Inf. in Iceland in June 1942. Went to England and Ireland where a mutual transfer was made and he became an aid man in 2nd Bn. Hit France July 10, 1944 and combat July 14. Finished as an aid man in G Co.

The Good Lord saw him through it all to the end of the war, and he was discharged Sept. 22, 1945.

Married Betty Jane Mateja on Sept. 6, 1947. They have two sons, Gary and Carl, and three grandchildren: Elizabeth,

Frederick and William. He retired from the post office as a carrier after 30 years. Moved to Florida in 1972 and drove a school bus. He retired after 10 and a half years and still works part-time. He lives in Wildwood, FL and keeps active in bowling. He is a member of the 10th Inf. Association, 5th Div. Society, VFW and American Legion.

DALE E. BARTON, entered the U.S. Army in November 1939 at Fort Logan, CO where he took his basic training with the 7th Engineers. Went to Fitzsimmons General Hospital in Denver on detached service for a short time. Then to Camp Grant at Rockford, IL with the 27th Training Bn. as an infantry drill instructor. He joined the 5th Div. at Fort Custer, MI in H Co., 10th Inf. Went on Louisiana maneuvers then back to Fort Custer.

Went to Iceland in January 1942 on the *Bournequeen*. Was there for about 18 months. While in Iceland, he became part of the 5th Medical Bn. Sailed to Liverpool, England on the *Samaria*. Was stationed at Tidworth Barracks, Salisbury, England. Later to Camp Ballywillwill at Castlewellan in North Ireland.

Sailed from Southampton, landing on Utah Beach after the invasion. Went to A Co., 11th Inf. under the company commander, Capt. Cooper. During Battle of the Bulge went to hospital in England on Dec. 25, 1944 for two months. Returned to service and was with the 45th Signal Corps until going home as soon as the war ended.

Discharged honorably at Ft. Logan, CO and returned to Iowa where he married Joanne Robins in 1946. They lived in several western areas, the last being Albuquerque, NM for 20 years. Worked for Yellow Freight System for 30 years, retiring in 1982. In 1991 they moved to their Iowa farm and are enjoying the country life. They had two daughters and one son: Rita, Beth and James. James was killed during the Vietnam War in Laos during a helicopter raid. They have five grandchildren.

JOSEPH E. BAYRUEM, joined the Army from his home town, Cincinnati, OH. Inducted at Fort Thomas, KY on Sept. 19, 1940. Basic training was at Fort Thomas with Co. G, 10th Inf. Moved to Fort Custer

and joined the 5th Div. and had more training.

Transferred to Co. L, 10th Inf. and left for Iceland in 1941. Spent 23 months in Iceland in a rifle company. Moved to England in 1943 and went into combat in 1944 in France. After three months of combat, he had 134 discharge points. Was honorably discharged at San Antonio, TX on Oct. 19, 1945 with the rank private first class.

LEON R. BELARDINELLI, was born in Chicago, IL on Dec. 20, 1916. Was drafted into the Army April 6, 1941 to do the one year of selective service, but Dec. 7, 1941 changed all that. From the induction center they went to Camp Grant near Rockford, IL. All their clothes and other items were issued there at the time. He was singled out by an officer who fitted him to a tee, even to the shoes, so that he looked like an officer. Later in the barracks it was bedlam as the rest of the fellows were exchanging clothes among themselves to get things that fit. Stayed at Camp Grant for three days; went to Fort Custer, MI; put in Co. I, 2nd Inf. where he remained until medical discharge on Feb. 6, 1946.

Went on maneuvers in Tennessee, Louisiana and Arkansas. They hiked 25 miles a day for 10 days, riding the rest of the way. On the last day of the 10 day maneuvers, Lt. Goethel (a new officer with Co. I) couldn't make it any further and dropped out, so Belardinelli thought if the lieutenant could drop out, he would too.

He will never forget Dec. 7, 1941. He was home on week-end pass and received a telegram to report back to Fort Sheridan. The 2nd Inf. was dispersed around several facilities in the mid-west to protect them from sabotage. He was with a group from Co. I who were sent to Fort Wayne, Detroit,

MI. The 10th and 11th Inf. of the 5th Div. had been shipped to Iceland prior to December 7 because they were regular Army. When they were ready to ship out they knew their destination would also be Iceland.

Shipped out in February 1942 on the USS *Bournequeen* and was seasick all the way to Iceland and beyond. Left Iceland in August 1943 for Tidworth Barracks, England. In October 1943 they went to Northern Ireland. He made friends with a family in Rostrevor (still corresponds with them and had a chance to visit with them in London in 1985 and 1987).

The big blow on France came July 7, 1943. Their first big battle was July 26 at Vidouville, France. They lost about 40-50 percent of their personnel that day and he went from private to staff sergeant. He helped six men across Highway #3, which was under fire, to safety; gave aid to two men who were wounded and waiting for medics; and carried a wounded buddy on his back, down stream to safety. He never gave a man a job that he wouldn't do himself; he always went first and made sure of their safety. He made a good staff sergeant and didn't lose a man.

When they attacked Gravolotte on September 9, he made himself second scout and Larry Wekman first scout. Near the top of the hill, Belardinelli was wounded and the rest of the men were pinned down in another position. When picked up by the medics, everything became quiet and the next thing he remembers was at the aid station when Dr. Romanski said those magic words, "You are going home." He was given an anesthetic and when he became conscious was being carried by two German soldiers. He asked himself, "When did I get captured." After looking around, he discovered he was still free and they were POWs.

Returned to the States in December 1944. Married Evelyn Jarocki on July 14, 1945. They met on a blind date in 1941 and had corresponded throughout the war. They have two sons, one daughter and five grandchildren. After the war he worked for Automatic Electric for 27 years as an inspector on telephone equipment. Retired in July 1974 due to complication from his war injuries. They lived in California for nine years, then returned to Illinois in 1983.

His hobbies are golfing, gardening, travelling, cards and home repair. Co. I still holds a reunion every year at Battle Creek, MI.

JACK H. BENDER, was born Jan. 31, 1915 in Chicago, IL and was inducted April 9, 1941.

Went to Fort Sheridan; assigned to 5th Div., 10th Inf. at Fort Custer on April 11, 1941 for training; then maneuvers in Tennessee. Transferred to 2nd Inf. in August 1941, went on maneuvers in Louisiana in September and the balance of year was spent in Fort Custer.

Moved to Fort Dix in January 1942 and shipped to Iceland for 18 months, then Tidbury, England and Rosstrevor, Ireland. Transferred to G-3, 5X near Newcastle County Down. Left for combat, arrived D+30 France and attached to 1st Army.

Joined the 3rd Army. Countries: France, Luxembourg, Germany and Czechoslovakia. Was member of Task Force Warnock (Fort Driant). He received the Bronze Star and was veteran of five battles. Discharged July 1, 1945 with 119 points.

Worked for Westinghouse Electric, Kraft Foods and National Can Corp. as engineer for a total of 50 years then retired. Married 45 years and has two sons and five grandchildren.

FRED P. BODY, was born Jan. 21, 1918 in Charlerois, PA. The family moved to Chicago in 1920 and he attended Chicago Public Schools, graduated from Carthage College in 1939, did post graduate work at Chicago Teachers' College and DePaul University.

Was inducted into Army July 3, 1942 at Ft. Sheridan, IL. Went to basic training with Co. B, 320th Med Bn., 95th Div. at Camp Swift, TX and Ft. Sam Houston, TX. Was commissioned second lieutenant, Medical Administration Corps on Aug. 18, 1943 at Camp Barkley, TX.

Joined 5th Div. in August 1944 and was assigned to Med. Det., 2nd Bn., 2nd Inf. During service with 5th Div., he received four Battle Stars for Northern France, Ardennes, Rhineland and Central Europe. He was awarded the Silver Star on May 1, 1945; Bronze Star, March 26, 1944; Bronze Star Cluster, Dec. 24, 1945; and Purple Heart, March 18, 1945.

Was released from active duty as first lieutenant at Camp Atterbury, IN on Dec. 4, 1945.

He retired in 1977 from Chicago Board of Education where he had been employed as a teacher and later as principal.

RAYMOND P. BOROWINSKI, was born Jan. 10, 1916 in Chicago, IL; graduated from high school, 1935; attended part-time evening school in mechanical drafting, Illinois Institute of Technology 1935-1939.

Was called for the Selective Service April 11, 1941; assigned to the 2nd Bn., 10th Inf. Regt., 5th Div. (Red Diamond) with maneuvers in Tennessee-Arkansas with the 2nd Bn., 2nd Inf. Regt., 5th Div.

Departed for Iceland on the USS *Munargo,* Feb. 19, 1942; relieved the British Command in the vicinity of Reykjavik. Was among a small cadre of men selected to return to the States to train more selectees.

Maneuvers in Louisiana with the 291st Inf. Regt of the 75th Div.; landed in Gourock, Scotland; then Southampton, England; boarded LST and went to Utah Beach, France; assigned to Intelligence Section of Service Co., 318th Inf. Regt., 80th Div. Worked with the 318th Combat Team, Fauquemont, France entered the Maginot Line (November 1944); moved to Saar Union, France to defend Luxemburg; relieved the 101st Airborne Div. surrounded in Bastogne, Belgium (December 1944).

Entered Germany, February 1945 and fought in the Siegfried Line; entered Braunau, Austria (May 6, 1945). Gen. Eisenhower issued order to cease all operation on May 9 and the Japanese surrendered Aug. 15, 1945.

Discharged Sept. 19, 1945 with rank master sergeant. He received the Good Conduct Medal, American Theater, European Theater with three Bronze Stars, Bronze Star Medal, WWII Victory Medal, Army Occupation Medal, American Campaign Medal and the Combat Infantry Badge.

He resumed his trade as engineering draftsman, never married, he lives in Mendota, IL and enjoys gardening and travelling.

GLENN A. BOWERS, was born on Sept. 24, 1948. He joined the Army in Baker, OR on Aug. 29, 1967. Served with G Trp., 2/3 ARC, 1st Armd. Div., Ft. Lewis; A Trp., 4/12 Cav., 5th Inf. Div. (Mech), Vietnam; B Trp., 6/1 Cav., 2nd Armd. Div., Ft. Hood, TX.

Combat operations at Massachusetts Bay, Utah Mesa, Wm. Glade, Idaho Canyon, and Iroquois Grove.

Memorable experiences: Battle of Cam Hung. He was loader. Right side of turret struck with B-40 rocket, killing gunner and wounding TC. Second rocket struck infantry sergeant riding on tank fender, killing him and wounding driver. Several soldiers outside of tank were wounded. Enemy was 27th NKA Regt. He received Bronze Star with V for actions that day. NVA 118 KIA.

Discharged Aug. 28, 1970 as specialist fifth class. Now works as senior armor instructor (SFC) for Idaho Army National Guard.

WARREN H. BOWSER, was born in Parkersburg, WV in 1921 and later moved to Belpre, OH where he graduated from high school. In September 1939. He enlisted in Co. D, 10th Inf. at Fort Hayes, Columbus, OH and received training at Fort McClelland, AL. Participated in maneuvers in Georgia and Louisiana. On Dec. 3, 1940 he moved to Fort Custer, MI.

In the initial force, he left the U.S. Sept. 5, 1941 for Iceland and remained there until August 1943. From Iceland to Tidworth Barracks, England where he was promoted to sergeant of heavy machine gun squad.

Moved to Newcastle, Northern Ireland in October 1943. Shortly after the Normandy Invasion in June 1944, he left Belfast for Utah Beach and Sallen, France. Having fought their way forward to Foret de Cerisy, they joined the 3rd Army in August commanded by Lt. Gen. George S. Patton Jr. Having crossed the Moselle River in the fighting for Metz, he was wounded September 13 near Arry, France. For this battle he was awarded the Silver Star for gallantry in action.

He was discharged Aug. 7, 1945. Was in campaigns of Normandy, Northern France, Rhineland, Ardennes and Central Europe. He is now retired in Belpre, OH.

MORRIS WILBUR BOYER, was born Aug. 7, 1913 at Liberty, IN and lived there through grade and high school. He had two uncles in the Army and enjoyed listening to their stories of Army life and knew at a very early age that he wanted to be a soldier too when he grew up.

He enlisted in the Army Aug. 16, 1933 at Ft. Benjamin Harrison, IN where he also had basic training. Was assigned to Co. C, 11th Inf. and became a platoon sergeant there. Transferred in 1940 to Ft. Custer, MI and was there until September 1942 when he was sent overseas.

Spent time in Ireland, Iceland and England before he went into combat. Was wounded Nov. 15, 1944 just outside of Metz, France and sent back to the States for surgery at Pearcy Jones Army Hospital in Battle Creek, MI. A metal plate was put in his head. After several weeks in the hospital, he was returned to active duty at Ft. Custer, MI. He was there until January 1947, then sent to Japan for 17 months.

Returned to the States and assigned to ROTC duty in Grand Rapids, MI for six years; transferred to Ft. Carson, CO for six months; then retired Nov. 30, 1954 with 21 and a half years of service. Was awarded the Bronze Star, Purple Heart and all the usual medals and ribbons.

Married Stella Ross April 12, 1941 and lived in Grand Rapids, MI. Went to work for John K. Burch Co. and retired in 1969. Boyer passed away Nov. 23, 1991 from a heart attack. *Submitted by his wife, Stella Ross Boyer.*

CHARLES BRIGHT JR., was born April 21, 1921 in Chanute, KS and was inducted Aug. 1, 1942. After six weeks basic training at Camp Robinson, AR, he went im-

mediately to Iceland with Co. G, 10th Inf., 5th Div.

Entered ETO via Ireland at Utah Beach. He was wounded three times: Sept. 8, 1944, Moselle River near Metz; Jan. 1, 1945, Luxembourg City; and Feb. 1, 1945, Sauer River Weilerbach. After three years, one month and 14 days, he returned home for the first time since his induction.

In 1956 he became a self-employed ditching contractor. Upon finishing school, his only child, a son, joined him in the business. Now, semi-retired, he and his wife of 51 years, live full time in a bus conversion. When they are not traveling he still likes to work at Bright's Ditching Inc. Chanute is still home base.

BYRON L. BROOKE, was born in Spring Valley, WI March 7, 1924. He joined the Army Reserve Dec. 11, 1942.

He was sent to Fort Sheridan April 23, 1943 for active duty then went to Fort Bragg, NC for basic training of 12 weeks on 105mm Howitzer.

Was given a 15 day leave just before being sent to Boston, then shipped out for England. Joined the 5th Inf. Div, went on to North Ireland for 10 months training. D-day + 33 they landed in France at Utah Beach; three weeks later they headed across France as part of Gen. Patton's 3rd Army.

After five major battles, they were in Wallern, Czechoslovakia on May 8, 1945, V-E day. End of campaign in Europe, then home to USA.

During 30 day leave, the A-bomb was dropped and war with Japan was over. Was discharged Oct. 13, 1945 at Fort Knox, KY.

Married Lois Hermansen in August 1946. He graduated from college in 1949 and taught and coached for 13 years. He sold Lutheran Brother Ins. for 25 years and is now retired. They have three children and three grandchildren.

GLENN C. BROWN, was born in Northern Wisconsin. He reported to Fort Sheridan, IL on April 12, 1943 for induction; was sent to Fort Bragg, NC for basic field artillery training; then to the 76th Inf. Div. in A.P. Hill, VA for field training.

In September 1943 was sent to England and assigned to the 50th FA BN, 5th Inf. Div. in Mourne Park, Kilkeel, Northern Ireland. Was with the 5th from then until seriously wounded in Karden West Germany on March 14, 1945. Was sent to 137th General Hospital in England April 28, 1945 for surgery and treatment. Returned to Kennedy General Hospital in Memphis, TN on June 12, 1945.

Was discharged Dec. 5, 1945 and worked for Fidelity Savings Bank, Antigo, WI for 11 years and First National Bank of Arizona for 19 years as branch manager. He is retired and lives in Scottsdale, AZ with his wife of 21 years, Angelina.

GEORGE E. BRYANT, was born in Tampa, FL on June 13, 1924. Was drafted from Lake City, FL in April 1943. Went to Camp Blanding, FL for induction into the Army. Basic training was at Camp Wheeler, GA.

Shipped overseas in October 1943 on the ship the *Empress of Australia*. Landed in Liverpool, England October 1943. Transferred to Co. L, 10th Inf., 5th Div. in November 1943. Was assigned to Co. L, 2nd Plt., 2nd Squad at Balleyed Mound Northern Ireland. Went to Normandy France July 6, 1944. Remained with the 2nd Plt., 2nd Squad until after they crossed the Rhine River March 24, 1945. He was a member of the patrol that raided Bettendorf Jan. 9, 1945. He remained in the Army for 20 years and retired in May 1963 to Magalia, CA. He received the Bronze Star Medal, Combat Infantry Badge, Expert M1 Rifle Badge, Good Conduct Medal, Commendation Medal and three campaign ribbons.

FRANK J. BUSZEK, was born 1917 in Detroit, MI and served with F Co., 2nd Inf., 5th Div. From July to November 1944, he was shot at, missed and hit a few times.

Once on Hill 313 was hit by a mortar shell in the upper left chest area, his field glasses saved his life. After locating the mortar position, the first sergeant, who got the glasses, asked what happened to them. He shook them and found a 1/2 inch piece of mortar shell in the glasses.

In or near the city of Reims, they were fired on by anti-aircraft guns (90mm point blank) from a high platform about 50 yards away. What helped them was two bomb craters. His men were wounded and he had to crawl to the other crater and give first aid. At daybreak, they went into Reims and on to Verdum and Metz. He was wounded at Metz and was transferred by air to England to the city of Exeter to hospital.

After his hospital stay, he was shipped to Manhein, Germany. His outfit's name was 1931 Labor Supervision Co. Located in the stall engineering building, they had POWs. The size of the troops were 500 Italians, 700 Russians, and finally, 700 German troops (all ranks). Was discharged with the rank tech sergeant MOS 502 in September 1945. Points 105.

He retired in 1992.

JOSEPH A. CHAVANNE, was born Hamburg, NY on Oct. 15, 1925; graduated from Gardenville High School, Gardenville, NY on June 18, 1944. Took his Army physical on July 18, 1944 and was inducted Aug. 30, 1944. Went to basic training at Fort Sill, OK in wire and communications.

Departed for ETO on Feb. 18, 1945. Arrived Liverpool, England on Feb. 27, 1945, traveled to Southhampton and crossed the English Channel Feb. 28, 1945. Joined C Btry., 46th FA, 5th Div. day after crossing Rhine River as a cannoneer on 105 Howitzer.

Received EAME Campaign, American Campaign, Army of Occupation and World War II Victory Medals. Departed July 8, 1945. Arrived USA July 16, 1945 for six weeks jungle warfare training at Camp Campbell, KY in preparation for duty in South Pacific. When war ended he remained stationed at Camp Campbell until receiving his ruptured duck from Fort Dix, NJ on July 2, 1946 as a battery supply staff sergeant.

After trying several jobs including about seven and a half years at the Buffalo, NY. Division of Westinghouse Electric as an inspector he joined the U.S. Post Office as a carrier retiring June 3, 1988 after 33 years service.

He is now spending his time with his wife Beatrice M. and adopted sons and daughters: Joseph G., Randy A., Sharon E. and Donna D. also with his 88 year old mother, Alice A., and grandchildren: Kim, Nat, Jeff, and Alicia. May God see fit to bless the good old USA.

THOMAS B. CLINE, was born in Sandusky, OH in 1924. Was drafted into the Army in 1943; took basic in Camp McCain, MS; shipped to Ireland to join C Co., 2nd Inf. Went to France with the rank private first class, was staff sergeant when he left and was wounded once. He received the Purple Heart, five Battle Stars and the Silver Star.

Went home to be a butcher in his father's slaughter house. Married Marguerite Angelo in 1950, a girl he graduated with in 1942. In 1951 he bought a semi-truck and hauled mostly military equipment in 48 states. In 1966 he started Pin Oak Lake Park (campground) on his father's farm (who passed away in 1964) for a hobby. It grew and grew and finally had to stop trucking. In 1976 he started Pin Oak RV Sales Inc. and sold it all in 1987.

Now traveling in Vogue motor home in winter, plus once in awhile in the summer. Has a few old cars and trucks to play with, raises chickens to eat, has a garden, mows a lot of grass and loves it. Life has been good to him. He has two successful children plus grandchildren.

CHARLES I. COCO, was born in Rochester, NY in November 1924. He joined the Army Feb. 27, 1943 and took basic training in Fort Bragg, NC. He was shipped to England and assigned in August 1943 with the A Btry., 21st FA BN, 5th Div. as ammunition handler for the 155 Howitzer. He went to Ireland and then to France for 10 months of combat with the 3rd Army.

Charles was sent back to the States in 1944 and discharged from Camp Atterbury, IN with the rank private first class.

Married his wife Amelia in 1946 and

raised two daughters and a son. They enjoy their six grandchildren. Worked for Pfaudler Company in Rochester, NY for 36 years. After retiring in 1986, he spends winter with his wife in Myrtle Beach, SC and summer in Rochester, NY.

WILLIAM COLON (BILL), entered the Army in February of 1942 and took basic training at Ft. McClellan, AL, then attended school at Ft. Benning, GA. Was briefly assigned to the 78th Div. at Camp Butner, NC, then sent overseas in October 1943.

Landed in Scotland and joined the 5th Div. in Northern Ireland, where he trained with the 11th Inf. They sailed for France in early July 1944 and served in Normandy, Brittany and across France to Metz. Was wounded and captured in September 1944 (two others were killed). Got patched up and sent to Stalag 7-A, a prison camp near Moosberg.

In April 1945 Stalag 7-A was evacuated and the POWs were marched away from advancing Allied forces. Colon and a friend slipped away and traveled by night toward the sound of guns, dodging retreating German forces. On April 30, 1945 they met elements of the 80th Div. and were free. Germany surrendered a week later.

THOMAS H. COOPER, received an ROTC commission as a second lieutenant, FA, upon graduation from the University of Illinois in 1940. Reported for duty with the 3rd Bn., 19th FA Regt. (later 50th FA BN) on July 5, 1940 at Camp McCoy, WI.

He served in Iceland and the European Theater of Operations for 41 months. He commanded Btry. A and served on the staff of the 50th FA BN during combat from Normandy to Czechoslovakia. With Capt. Herman Jost and two enlisted men, he captured 64 German soldiers at Metz, France.

Cooper stayed in the Army after WWII and retired as a colonel in 1972 after 32 years of service. One of his most interesting assignments was to command a unit which provided nuclear weapons to NATO allies: British, German, French, Dutch, Belgian, Greek and Turkish forces.

Tom married Mary Hall in 1941, and they now reside in Mesa, AZ

LACY OTHA DAVIS JR., was born and raised on a farm in Marshall County, AL on April 10, 1948. Was drafted into the Army on March 13, 1968; basic training at Ft. Benning, GA; AIT at Ft. Dix, NJ then to Ft. Carson, CO where he volunteered for Vietnam.

Arrived Vietnam on Aug. 28, 1968, Con Thien 1st Brigade, 61st Inf. Div., 5th Inf. Mech., Charlie Co., 2nd Plt., 3rd Sqdn., point man. Walked point on DMZ from the Ho Chi Mein Trail to the South China Sea. Operated Bi Long Valley, Ashau U Khe Sonh Valley (July 16-Aug. 21, 1969).

He was one of the Bloody Red Devils. Their battles were many with very little rest. They patrolled the DMZ setting ambushes, while being ambushed and living in fox holes.

After seven days of R&R in Japan, he left Khe Sonh for the States. Received honorable discharge March 13, 1970.

ARCADIO GARCIA DEVERA, was born in the Philippine Islands on Nov. 9, 1909. Went to ROTC School and trained in Camp Roberts, CA. He went home and was called back to duty after Pearl Harbor. Reported in at Ft. Sheridan on Jan. 19, 1942. Was assigned to C Co., 11th Regt., 5th Div. and stayed with unit until discharge.

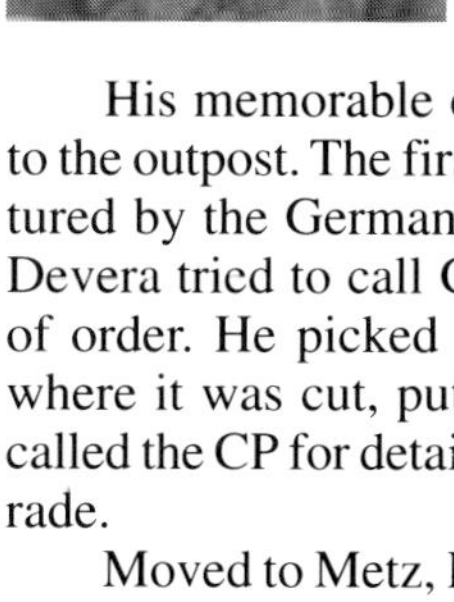

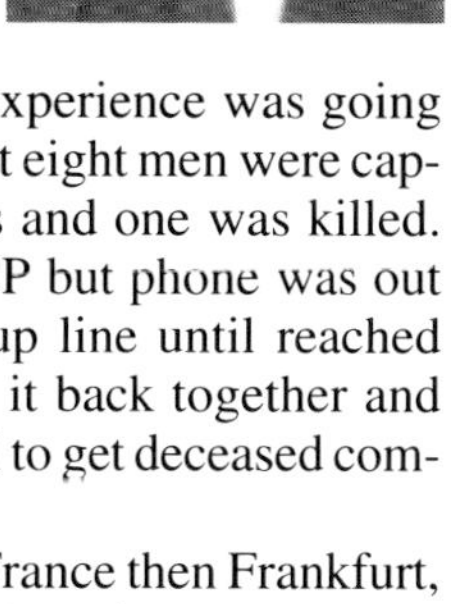

His memorable experience was going to the outpost. The first eight men were captured by the Germans and one was killed. Devera tried to call CP but phone was out of order. He picked up line until reached where it was cut, put it back together and called the CP for detail to get deceased comrade.

Moved to Metz, France then Frankfurt, Germany and then to Austria.

Was discharged June 19, 1945 with the rank of T-4 grade. He received five Battle Stars, Combat Badge and the Bronze Star.

He is now enjoying the life of retirement.

RANDOLPH C. DICKENS, was born at Statesboro, GA on Nov. 15, 1914 and was raised in Lake City, FL. He graduated from the U.S. Military Academy, West Point, New York on June 12, 1936 and was commissioned a second lieutenant of infantry.

Served with 1st Bn., 2nd Inf. (August 1940). Commander 3rd Bn. (1942-1943). 5th Inf. Div. Assistant Chief of Staff, G-3 (1943-1945).

Battles participated in: Normandy, Saint Lo breakthrough, pursuit across France, reduction of Metz, Bulge, Siegfried Line, first Allied Force Division to cross the Rhine, Ruhr Pocket, Southern Germany, Vietnam (1st Inf. Div.) 1965-1966.

Retired from the U.S. Army in 1966 with the rank brigadier general. He received the Distinguished Service Medal, Silver Star, Legion of Merit and the Bronze Star.

Has master's degree (mathematics) Duke 1967; Doctor of Education, North Carolina State University, 1973; Dean of Continuing Education, Fayetteville State University, 1973-1979; mathematics instructor at North Carolina State University, 1967-1973 and from 1979-1988. He retired in 1988.

JAMES N. DOLAN, was born Oct. 3, 1916 in Jackson, MI. He joined the service April 1, 1940 and served with 21st FA to HQ MP Co., Fort Custer, MI.

Was part of the company that kept Iceland secured from the Germans. Memorable experience was the many conflicts that the company had to break up during the R&R.

Discharged from Schick General Hospital, Clinton, IA, December 1944 from wounds inflicted in Iceland. He achieved the rank of sergeant.

He lives alone with his best pal, Shep, in retirement. His hobby is keeping in touch with his many friends on the two-way radio.

ROBERT M. DUFFY, was born June 15, 1918 at Wilkesville, OH. He was inducted into the U.S. Army at Fort Knox, KY

on Oct. 15, 1940. He was trained at Ft. Knox, served with the 46th FA BN in all the European battles, achieving the rank of staff sergeant as the 46th FA BN radio sergeant.

His memorable experience was the time the 3rd Army ran out of gas, the 46th FA was in the little village of Lorry before Metz. The Germans would shell them about every night and day from the forts around Metz. One of those nights a friend of his was nearing the house where he slept. When he heard a barrage coming, he dove for the door and his helmet came off and rolled down the long hall where another soldier was sleeping on the floor. The sleeping soldier raised up and said, "It must have been a dud."

Received honorable discharge at Camp Atterbury, IN on June 21, 1945.

After his discharge he attended a school for refrigeration and air conditioning in Chicago, IL on the GI bill. He worked at this vocation for three and a half years in his hometown of Jackson, OH. He went on to work as a radio and electronic technician in Gallipolis, OH. In 1954 he began working at the Goodyear Atomic Plant and retired from there 29 years later as a physicist. His hobbies include gardening, playing gospel music and travelling with his wife, Helen, to visit their children. He is also a ham radio operator with the call letters KB8PM.

ROBERT J. DUNSIRN, was born in Appleton, WI on Sept. 10, 1920. He enlisted in the U.S. Army on Nov. 4, 1940. Bob took basic training and was stationed with HG Co., 1st Bn., 2nd Inf., 5th Inf. Div. at Fort Sheridan, IL. He was then sent with his unit to Fort Custer, MI and was in the 1940-1941 Army maneuvers.

On Feb. 19, 1942 his unit was on the ship USS *Macauley* and arrived at Reykjavik, Iceland on April 17, 1942 and was stationed at Camp MacArthur. He left Iceland Aug. 6, 1943 for England and was stationed in Wiltshire, England in the Tidworth Barracks. In late October 1943, he was sent to Northern Ireland south in the Newery area at which time special training took place, many field exercises, vigorous marches and more so until his unit was combat ready.

On June 29, 1944 he was on ship with his unit and arrived off the coast of Normandy. On July 13, 1944 Dunsirn found himself in the heart of combat and saw many of his unit wounded and killed in action. So many stories could be told of these experiences from Normandy to Germany. He was staff sergeant in charge of communications.

Dunsirn was captured by the Germans and wounded on the night of March 22; he had been across the Rhine River on a jeep that was destroyed by enemy fire from a unit of about 150 Germans that had come down the road and opened fire. A few weeks later American troops came and took over the make shift German hospital and Dunsirn was sent to France for shrapnel operations. He was then sent to LaHarve on June 15, 1945.

He was sent home after five years of service, three of which was spent overseas without any home leave. He was awarded many medals including the Purple Heart, Cluster, Bronze Star, Combat Infantry Badge and others. He was discharged Aug. 19, 1945 from Fort Sheridan, IL.

Dunsirn is now retired from the company he and his partner, Don Buchta, built from the ground up, Mid America Tag & Label Company. He still keeps himself busy doing consulting work for the Tag & Lable industry. He has two sons, Duane and Brian; daughter, Janis (by their mother, Agnes Kutz Dunsirn); and 11 wonderful grandchildren. Dunsirn has shared and enjoyed last 16 years with Carol Ann Dunsirn.

RICHARD H. DURST (DICK), was born and raised in Akron, OH, graduating from its university during June of 1940. He joined the 11th Inf. Regt. at Fort Harrison, IN and remained with it in the States, Iceland, England, Northern Ireland and Europe until early 1945 when he was seriously wounded while leading Co. G across the Sauer River near Echternach, Luxembourg.

He returned to active duty 16 months later to serve in various capacities within the U.S., Austria, Vietnam and Paraguay until June of 1965.

Dick returned to Purdue University for post-graduate studies immediately after his retirement and subsequently served as Dean

at Salem College and St. John's Military Academy.

His military decorations include the Silver Star, Bronze Star, Purple Heart, Army Commendation Medal and the Combat Infantry Badge.

He currently resides in Akron, OH with his wife, Helen.

KENNETH L. EKWALL, was born in Shickley, NE on June 6, 1913. He was drafted into the U.S. Army April 1941 in Chicago with basic training in 46th FA BN at Ft. Custer. He participated in Tennessee and Louisiana maneuvers and artillery firing at Camp McCoy.

Transferred to 5th Div. Arty. HQ going to Iceland in May 1942. He served in the U.S. Army Forces Tactical School HQ under Col. Douglas Crane, School Commander.

Ekwall returned to the States in October 1942 to enter Quartermaster OCS with promotion to second lieutenant in February 1943. He served in Columbus ASF Depot, Okinawa and Korean occupation, entering reserve status February 1946.

Was employed by Western Electric Co. in Lincoln and Omaha until retiring in 1976 with the rank lieutenant colonel, USA (RET). He and his wife, Frances, have two daughters and five grandchildren.

DOUGLAS R. ENGBLOM, was born June 28, 1924 in Royal Oak, MI. Was inducted March 5, 1943 and served in C Btry., 19th FA BN, 5th Div.

Trained at Ft. Sill, OK and fought in battles in Normandy, Northern France, Ardennes, Rhineland and Central Europe.

His memorable experience was meeting his brother from the 4th Div. in the combat area.

Received honorable discharge Oct. 6, 1945 with the rank T-4.

Today he is retired, but still works part-time.

MELVIN M. ESAREY, was born in Beechwood, IN and grew up in Southern Illinois. He entered the Army in June 1941 and had basic training in field artillery at Ft. Sill, OK. He was sent to Ft. Custer, Battle Creek, MI and was assigned to HQ Btry., 21st FA BN, 5th Inf. Div.

The 21st went to Iceland in April 1942. HQ Btry. was stationed at Colne Valley, a camp east of Reykjavik. The outfit spent alternate months training and working at supply depots, unloading ships, etc.

He applied for Officer Candidate School and was sent to Ft. Sill in January 1943 after crossing the North Atlantic during a December storm. The convoy was two weeks late and was diverted to Halifax, Nova Scotia.

After OCS he was assigned as survey officer (and, later, as air observer) to HQ Btry., 358th FA BN, 95th Inf. Div. After Louisiana maneuvers, desert maneuvers and mountain maneuvers, the 95th was sent to the ETO and assigned to Patton's 3rd Army. Later in the war, it went to the 9th Army. Esarey served in the ETO from August 1944 to the end of the war.

He participated in campaigns at Metz, Moselle River, Saarlautern, Saar River, Linnich, Roar River, Duisburg, Rhine River, and the Ruhr Pocket. He was awarded the Bronze Star, Medaille De Metz and the Air Medal.

Was relieved from active duty on Dec. 7, 1945 and was transferred to the Active Reserve, where he later commanded a reserve unit until 1956.

After the war he became a high school driver education teacher and taught some 6,500 young people to drive. He was co-author of a driver education textbook. Now is enjoying retirement.

FOSTER FERGUSON, was born November 1920 in Morgan County, KY. Was drafted August 1942 and went to basic at Camp Wheeler, GA. Sent to Iceland and assigned to Co. B, 11th Inf., 5th Div.

Went to Tidworth England; New Castle

Northern Ireland; France in early July 1944. He fought in many battles: Angers, Fort Driant, Metz, Bitburg, Gross-Grau and crossed many rivers. The Moselle River being the worst. He was the first man across the mighty Rhine at the Oppenheim Crossing. The bitter cold weather at the Battle of the Bulge played a big part in the amount of casualties.

Received honorable discharge Oct. 2, 1945 with the rank tech sergeant platoon sergeant of the 2nd Plt. of Co. B.

He became a truck driver for suburban motor freight in Columbus, OH. Retired in 1978 after having a heart attack.

ROBERT W. FIRLIK, was born in Grand Rapids, MI on June 21, 1921. He enlisted in the Army on Sept. 12, 1939, just after the Germans invaded Poland. He took recruit drill at Fort Brady, MI in Co. M, 2nd Inf. Regt., 3rd Bn., 2nd Inf. and was assigned to guard the Sault Sainte Marie canals or locks at the rapids of the St. Mary's River connecting Lake Superior and Lake Huron.

After the 5th Div. was reactivated in October of 1939, he went to Fort McClellan, AL to be with the 2nd Inf. Regt. when it joined the 10th and 11th Inf. Regts. to make the 5th Div., reorganized, of triangular type. Subsequently, from the day of his enlistment to the day of his discharge, Sept. 4, 1945, he served in companies: M, A, D and F of the 3rd, 1st and 2nd Bns. of the regiment with a 10 week stint of detached service with the MP at Fort Sheridan, IL in late 1940.

A qualified combat infantryman, he trained selectees at Fort Custer, MI; served and trained in Iceland and Tidworth Barracks, England as well as in the north of Ireland for the imminent invasion of Normandy.

After the landing was made by the gallant troops which proceeded them a month earlier, the 2nd Inf. came in at Utah Beach on July 9, 1944 and within hours began to carry out orders to relieve the 16th Inf. Regt. of the 1st Div. From that moment the 2nd Inf., 5th Div. was firmly resolved to the complete liberation of Europe. It was brought into Gen. George S. Patton's 3rd Army and never stopped until the European Theater was completely secure and the Germans had surrendered on May 8, 1945.

During six years of service, 42 months of overseas duty, Firlik achieved the rank of staff sergeant. He earned the American Defense, American Campaign, European Campaign with Silver Service Star, Good Conduct, Army of Occupation, Combat Infantryman's Badge, (Austria) the Victory as well as the Bronze Star Medals. Participated in the battles for Normandy, Northern France, Ardennes, Rhineland and Central Europe.

Married Shirley Jean Dygert in December 1940. They have two sons, two lovely daughters-in-law, a beautiful granddaughter and four handsome grandsons. Firlik worked 27 years for Eaton Corp., the last 10 years as director of marketing research.

He is retired and enjoying his family, the Ohio State University Buckeyes (win or lose) and traveling. He and Shirley have returned to most of the places at which he served while overseas. On the 40th Anniversary of D-day, thanks to Henry and Monique Feyereisen of Foetz, Luxembourg, they toured the beaches of Normandy and retraced the march of the 2nd Inf. from Vidouville through France and Germany. Henry Feyereisen had served as a freedom fighter in the underground during the German Occupation of Luxembourg. Gen. George S. Patton and his command staff used the home of Monique's parents for their HQ from which to conduct the Ardennes Offensive during the Battle of the Bulge.

RICHARD J. FREY, was born near Millersville, Lancaster County, PA. He entered the service March 1943 and went to basic training at Fort Sill, OK and Camp Shelby, MS.

Was shipped to England and joined Btry. B, 19th FA BN. Next went to Northern Ireland for more training. Entered the war zone on July 9, 1944 on the Normandy Coast. He served as radio operator and jeep driver with forward observer until the end of the war.

Discharged from 5th Div. at Camp Campbell, KY in October 1945. He received five Battle Stars and Bronze Star. He had a T-5 rating.

Started training in architectural drafting, eventually became a registered architect in Pennsylvania. He married in 1947 and has four married daughters and eight grandchildren. Employed by Albright and Friel, Philadelphia; Buchart Engineering, York, PA; Henry Y. Shaub, Architect; and Armstrong World Ind. in Lancaster, PA for over 26 years. Retired Jan. 1, 1989 and lives in Millersville, PA.

MERLE HARLON GARDNER, was born in Syracuse, NY on July 24, 1916. He enlisted in the U.S. Army in 1943 and took basic at Orlando, FL. He was assigned to the 3rd Army, 5th Div. under Gen. Patton. Was also stationed at Camp Edwards, MA and Augusta, GA. Was in numerous conflicts at the Battle of the Rhine River and Luxembourg.

Other countries he fought in were Czechoslovakia, Germany, and France. During this time he was awarded the Good Conduct Medal, three Battle Stars, Infantry Combat Badge and Bronze Star. He was discharged in August 1945 after achieving the rank of corporal.

Married Hilda Loomis on Nov. 23, 1940 and had three children: David Lee, Gerald Allen, Janet Louise and five grandchildren. He was employed at Roleway Bearing and retired in 1978 after 46 years with the company. His leisure time is spent on the lake fishing and in the woods hunting. He currently resides in Dexter, NY.

MARTIN J. GEMOETS, was born in El Paso, TX on July 7, 1914. He enlisted in the Army in September 1942; graduated from OCS in 1943 and joined the 5th Inf. Div. as a replacement rifle platoon leader in October 1944. Served as platoon leader and executive officer in I Co., executive officer in K Co. and CO of L Co.

Discharged in March 1946, he received the Purple Heart with OLC, Bronze Star with OLC and V and the Combat Infantry Badge. Was recalled to active duty during the Korean War. Retired in 1974 with the rank of colonel after 32 years of active and reserve duty.

Married in 1937 to present wife, Doris Krueger, of El Paso, TX. They have two children and three grandsons. Previously, he was employed by the FBI, U.S. Customs Service and the Veterans Administration. While in private business he was the president of O.K. Van and Storage Company of New Mexico and Texas. Presently he is retired and lives in Las Cruces, NM and utilizes his time in golfing, traveling, reading and being a do-gooder.

JACK S. GERRIE, was commander of Co. G, 11th Inf. Regt. Gerrie had survived many grim and dangerous engagements as he and his men spearheaded Gen. Patton's 3rd Army all the way across France after the landing at St. Mere Egllse. They made the dramatic break-through at St. Lo, crossed the Seine near Fontaineblau, the Marne in the vicinity of Epernay and finally the Moselle at Dornot.

There in the Metz area in early September, they reached a point farther east than any other allied troops had achieved on the western front. On that long trek and in the climax battles at Fort Driant and the Moselle crossing, Capt. Gerrie's leadership was so brilliant and his heroism so pronounced that he won the Distinguished Service Cross, Bronze Star Medal, Croix de Guerre with Palm Leaf and the Purple Heart before his death.

Captain S. Gerrie was the son of Mr. and Mrs. Chester A. Gerrie of Ripon, WI and one of the outstanding athletes of his college generation. He entered active service in June 1941 and died December 1944. *Submitted by Joseph Pietroforte.*

FREDERICK J. GILL, was born July 1925 in Passaic, NJ. He was inducted in August 1943, Newark, NJ and went to basic training with 63rd Inf. Div. at Camp Van Dorn, MS.

Sent to ETO and assigned to Co. B, 2nd Inf., 5th Div. Participated in Normandy, Northern France and Rhineland campaigns, the hedgerows at St. Lo, Metz, etc. Was wounded Nov. 11, 1944 and returned home to be discharged in December 1945.

Married with two grown children. Was a bus driver most of his working life. Retired August 1987. He is active with Military Order of the Purple Heart and DAV. He takes great pride in being a veteran of the 5th Inf. Div., the greatest outfit in the world.

MARK C. GOODMAN JR., was born in Chicago, IL in 1924 and inducted into the U.S. Army April 28, 1943. He went to basic at Camp Croft, Spartensburg, SC. Joined the 5th Inf. Div. at Newcastle, North Ireland on Oct. 21, 1943. Served in Co. A, 10th Inf. Regt. until Oct. 31, 1945.

Landed in France July 6, 1944 and earned five Bronze Stars on European Theater of Operations Ribbon for combat in Normandy, Northern France, Rhineland, Central Europe and the Ardennes. Was awarded Bronze Star Medal, Combat Infantryman Badge and the Good Conduct Medal.

Received BS degree at the University of Illinois. Married Joan Turza, they have three children: Maura, Mia and Mark. He manufactured and distributed ice cream and frozen foods. He is author of Co. A 10th Inf. Combat narrative.

MARDEN R. GOODWIN, was born in Chicago, IL on Oct. 26, 1918. Was inducted into the service July 9, 1941. Assigned to 3rd Armd. Div. at Camp Polk, LA. On cadre to the 7th Armd. Div. as sergeant. On cadre to the 11th Armd. Div. as technical sergeant, CCA (Operations and Communications).

Graduated Infantry OCS, Ft. Benning, GA on Aug. 4, 1943. Attended Officers Communications School, Ft. Benning, GA. Taught IRTC at Camp Wheeler, GA. Arrived England Aug. 23, 1944. Retrained specialists for infantry duty while in England. Infantry unit commander, M Co., 2nd Inf. Regt., 5th Inf. Div., Dec. 1, 1944. General Kilburn sent Goodwin back with the 11th Armd. Div. on Feb. 7, 1945. Division signal supply officer, 151st Armd. Signal Co. Transferred to 26th Inf. Div. when the 11th was dissolved in Austria.

Returned to the U.S. at the end of 1945.

Separated from the service as first lieutenant on Feb. 22, 1946. He received the Combat Infantry Badge, EAME Ribbon, ETO Ribbon with three Bronze Stars, Good Conduct Medal, American Theater Ribbon, WWII Victory Medal, Expert with Rifle, and two Overseas Service Bars.

Spent the majority of his working life as a manufacturers representative. Presently he is retired and living in Miami, FL.

BILLY R. HALL, was born Aug. 16, 1925 at Crothersville, IN. Was drafted and entered the Army Nov. 27, 1943 at Ft. Thomas, KY. He took basic training at Camp Croft, SC, December 1943-March 1944. After furlough was en route to Camp Kilmer, NJ.

Left the States on June 6, 1944 and arrived in England four days later. Arrived in France June 29, 1944, joined 2nd Inf., AT Co. on July 16, 1944, 1st Army. After break through from Normandy, became part of 3rd Army.

Dobbins, Dunsmore and Hall took basic together and ended up in same platoon, although not always in same replacement depots. Campaigns were Normandy, Northern France, Rhineland, Ardennes and Central Europe.

Most memorable was the Rhine River crossing by 5th Div.; hedgerows in Normandy; forts at Metz; hardships during Battle of Bulge; meeting Ernest Hemmingway and French FFI at Ramboillet, France; and being in Czechoslovakia on V-E day.

Was honorably discharged at Camp Atterbury, IN on Dec. 7, 1945 with the T-5 rank.

Married Mary in 1946, they have three children. He retired in 1987 after 42 years with Arvin Industries Inc., Columbus, IN. He enjoys sports and working outdoors.

JOSEPH HASLINGER, was born in Fremont, OH in 1916. He enlisted in the U.S. Army on Nov. 24, 1940 and took basic at Ft. Benjamin Harrison. He joined the 11th Inf. and was assigned to Co. C. From Ft. Custer went on maneuvers at Tennessee and Louisiana. He became the company cook.

After several months at Ft. Sheridan, he returned to Ft. Custer and was assigned

to Co. L. In April 1942 they left for Reykjavik, Iceland, spent 15 months there and became T-4 sergeant. Spent four months at Tidsworth, England, then to Ballikinder, Ireland. On July 6, 1944 he went to Omaha Beach, Normandy. His tour of duty consisted of Luxembourg, Germany, Austria and Czechoslovakia.

After a year in combat, he was discharged on the point system. He returned home to his orchard farm in 1945 and joined the carpenter union. In 1946 he married Mardel Shammo, they have six children, 18 grandchildren and one great-grandchild.

WILFRID H. HAUGHEY JR., was born in Battle Creek, MI in 1910. Was commissioned second lieutenant from ROTC. Began active duty April 1941 in D Co., 10th Inf. Regt., 5th Inf. Div. at Ft. Custer, MI. His entire active duty service, until separated in January 1946, was with the 10th Inf. Regt.

Left the States in September 1941 for Iceland, the troops spent two years, primarily as labor unloading provisions from military supply ships for the Armed Forces. Transferred to England for three months for new equipment and training.

Sent to Northern Ireland for nine months of intensive training. Haughey landed in Normandy D + 33 days as executive officer 1st Bn. and fought through France. He assumed command of 1st Bn. Sept. 9, 1944 just before assault crossing of Moselle River at Arnaville, France. Continued through Germany and assumed command of 3rd Bn. Feb. 9, 1945, fought on through Luxembourg, Austria and Czechoslovakia with Patton's 3rd Army until the end of war in Europe.

Promoted to lieutenant colonel on June 7, 1945. Haughey's tour of duty in WWII was four years, nine months and five days, including 47 months overseas without home leave. Participated in Normandy, Northern France, Ardennes, Rhineland and Central Europe campaigns. He spent 275 days in contact with the enemy. Adjusted service rating, 157 points.

He received the Distinguished Service Cross, Silver Star, Bronze Star and the Combat Infantry Badge.

RAYMOND A. HERNANDEZ, was born March 19, 1926 and grew up in Yonkers, NJ. Upon graduation he went into the Army and spent four months basic training at Camp Croft, SC. As an infantry replacement, he joined Co. E, 2nd Inf. at Diekirch, Luxembourg in January 1945.

Participated in Rhineland Campaign, then at Ruhr Pocket, Frankfurt, and hundreds of miles on Gen. Patton's tanks and trucks to Czechoslovakia and the end of the European war. During that period he was a bazooka man, platoon runner and rifleman in the 3rd Squad.

Memorable experiences: was made platoon runner and with his walkie talkie had to be with the platoon leader at all times. They had a little house and he was in bed on the side against the wall. The lieutenant came back from a meeting at company headquarters and got into his side of the bed. Like many others he seemed to be always plagued with that illness. In the middle of the night he had to get out of bed fast, but did not quite make it over the lieutenants sleeping form. Next morning he was transferred to the 3rd Squad as a rifleman. (He doesn't blame the lieutenant for firing him, he would have done the same.) Another time in a town they were clearing Germans out of attics and basements when they took the town. He was coming down the stairs from the attic, another guy was just ahead of him, Hernandez tripped and fell into him, knocking him down and they both tumbled down to the first floor. His carbine hit the wall and got off a round. (Yes, carbine, it was lighter, in fact, more than half the platoon had Tommy guns, swapped their M-1s with tankers who wanted rifles to keep the enemy bazooka men at bay. That got changed soon after.) The bullet hit the guy in front of him in the foot, the fleshy part the heel. He had just returned from the hospital with trench foot and was complaining that it was not cured. So, a billion dollar wound, but half a dozen guys witnessed it, so Hernandez was not charged with deliberately doing it.

A day before leaving, the whole 2nd Inf. on the boat to come home, orders listed everyone, about 240 men in the company by rank. There were five privates, four yard birds who were let out of the stockade to fill up the company and Hernandez. He complained to the company commander and in the afternoon a special order came out and Hernandez was promoted to private first class. The reason he was not promoted before, well the first sergeant told the captain that he never did believe that story that Hernandez did not deliberately shoot the man in the foot.

Another year was spent at Camp Campbell, KY, then discharged on points. While there he was company clerk, then battalion clerk, then battalion sergeant major (rank T/5) as he did not wish to re-enlist.

Has a small business and not yet retired. Will probably soon turn the business over to his son and maybe work part-time. He has two other children and four grandchildren living in Alaska.

LEROY W. HOON, was born Feb. 29, 1920 in Steelton, PA. He was drafted in December 1941 and was inducted Jan. 6, 1942. Took basic at Camp Wheeler, GA, then transferred to Battle Creek, MI and was assigned to the 5th Inf. Div., 11th Inf. Regt. C Co.

Left for Iceland in April 1942. This was the beginning of a 42 month tour of duty overseas which included 10 moths of combat duty. He also served in England, Ireland, France, Luxembourg, Germany and Austria.

After the invasion, their unit was transferred to Patton's 3rd Army and on July 13, 1944, they relieved the 26th Inf., 1st Div. at Caumont, France. In July 1945 he was temporarily transferred to Shaef HQ.

Discharged Nov. 22, 1945. He married Dora Kroh in 1946, they have two sons, two daughters and seven grandchildren. He is a retired tool designer.

WILBUR J. HOOPER, was born in West Point, VA on Feb. 28, 1923. He was inducted in the U.S. Army on March 29, 1943 and took basic at Ft. Bragg, NC. Was assigned to the 21st FA BN, 5th Div., 3rd Army. 1943-1945 was spent in Ireland, Normandy, Northern France, Rhineland, Central Europe and the Ardennes. A memorable experience was the Battle of the Bulge.

Was discharged Oct. 9, 1945 and achieved the rank of first sergeant.

Married on July 21, 1945 to Catherine Lee while on furlough. They have one daugher, Kay Camp, a grandson and a granddaughter.

He is employed by the Chesapeake Corp. (Kraft Paper Mill) for 47 years and was assistant superintendent of the paper mill at his retirement in 1988. Leisure time is spent in a wood shop at his home, building and repairing for family, friends and church. Also enjoys traveling and attending furnishing transportation for grandchildren's activities.

WILLIAM T. HOPE, was born in Charlotte, NC. He was inducted into the Army on Oct. 18, 1941 at Ft. Bragg, NC and took basic training at Camp Croft, SC. Was then assigned to Co. H, 11th Inf. at Ft. Custer, MI.

Served in Iceland, England and took combat training in Northern Ireland. Landed on Utah Beach, Normandy, France on July 9, 1944. Was squad leader in the mortar platoon with the rank of staff sergeant. Participated in Normandy, Northern France, Rhineland, Ardennes and Central Europe campaigns.

After V-E day he was transferred to the 103rd Inf. Div. and returned to Fort Bragg, NC.

Was discharged Sept. 2, 1945 and earned the Combat Infantry Badge, EAMET Campaign Medal with five Bronze Service Stars, Purple Heart, American Defense Service Medal, Bronze Star Medal and the Good Conduct Medal.

He and wife, June, have been married since Feb. 23, 1946. They have a son, two daughters and five grandchildren. He retired in 1985 and enjoys traveling with June. They went to Europe in 1989 and revisited some of the old battle sites.

NORMAN T. HOWELL, was born on June 25, 1919 on a farm in Stanton, MI. Was drafted into the Army on April 2, 1941; joined 5th Div., 5th Sig. Co. at Ft. Custer; took maneuvers in Tennessee and Louisiana.

Served 14 months in Iceland, then to England then Ireland. Went into France 13 days after D-day. Attached to 1st Army a short time then to the 3rd Army until the end of war. Was transferred to 103rd Div., Sig. Co. in Insbrook Austria in June 1945 then back to States.

Discharged on Aug. 11, 1945 in Indiantown Gap, PA on Aug. 13, 1945 as a buck sergeant.

Worked for Ford Dealer 18 years in Stanton, MI then was a Massey Ferguson dealer for 14 years in Shepherd, MI. Married and has three children. Now he is retired and lives in Shepherd, MI.

THURMAN A. HUDDLESTON, was born Feb. 4, 1922 in Ligget, KY. He enlisted Oct. 17, 1939 at Ft. Thomas, KY and was assigned to Co. L, 10th Inf. Trained there and following Ft. McCellan, AL. The 5th Div. was reactivated and became his only unit during his duration.

Stationed at Ft. Benning, GA; Camp Polk, LA; Ft. Knox, KY; Camp Forrest, TN; Iceland, England and North Ireland. Iceland was the most memorable experience and the Aurora Borelis.

Was wounded in France and spent four a half months in hospitals in England. Then was returned to France. Never did rejoin his company, he did guard duty on German prisoners. With the point system he had 145 points, left Antwerp, Belgium for home turf.

Arrived Hampton Road, VA, went to Iceland Sept. 16, 1941 on the USS *Harry Lee*, arrived back on the McKinly Bovard

Aug. 6, 1945. Was discharged Aug. 12, 1945 with the rank tech sergeant.

He retired from American Cyanamid in March 1985. Moved to Tennessee where he enjoys whittling and wood carving.

HARRIS R. HUDSON, was born in Elyria, OH on May 16, 1918. One of the first draftees inducted in Columbus, OH on Feb. 14, 1941. He served in the 201st West Virginia Nat. Guard, 2nd Inf., Co. G, 5th Div., 503rd MP BN, Co. A.

Trained in Ft. Custer, MI, Iceland, England and Northern Ireland. Participated in combat in all the battles in the ETO from Normandy until the end of the war.

A memorable experience was serving with other soldiers in Gen. Patton's 3rd Army HQ. He received the Bronze Star and the Purple Heart.

He lives with his wife (who waited three and half years for him to return from the service) in Winter Park, FL. They were married July 7, 1945 and have a daughter and two granddaughters. He is now retired from U.S. Customs and spends his leisure time on gardening and reading.

CARL J. HUMMITZSCH, was born in Sheboygan, WI in 1918. Was drafted into the Army in May 1944. Basic was at Camp Blanding, FL in the infantry.

Left for overseas on Nov. 15, 1944 and landed at LeHarve. Was assigned to 10th Regt. on Dec. 11. Served five months in combat in Germany, Ruhr Pocket and Battle of the Bulge.

Prior to combat on December 16, he was standing guard duty with Pvt. Reynolds. One of their own men had a grudge against Reynolds and shot and killed him.

They held church services when they could. First Sgt. Sapp and Russel Hickman would conduct. Hummitzsch played the piano if one was available. In a church or on a hillside, usually about 100 attended.

Discharged Nov. 25, 1945, he received a Bronze Star.Married Sally in 1938, they have two daughters, Nancy and Peggy, and a son, Dennis. Also six grandchildren and two great-grandchildren.

GEORGE HENRY JACKSON, was born April 26, 1925 in Philadelphia, PA and entered the service June 5, 1943 at Ft. Thomas, KY. Served at Ft. Bliss, TX, 575th AAASP; 13th Abn., Ft. Bliss, TX; 174th Inf., Camp Chaffee, AR; Ft. Meade, MD; Camp Miles Standish, MA. Boston to Liverpool to Staunton, England; South Hampton to Normandy Beach.

First part of September 1944 5th Div., 1st Scout, 3rd Sqdn., 3rd Plt., F Co., 2nd Regt. Was shot on Dec. 24, 1944. Two days back with company kitchen and back to squadron. Evacuated latter part of February 1945 to hospital in Cheltenham, England.

8th Air Force to 100th Bomb Group, 3AD HQ and then to 418th Bomb Sqdn. as motor pool driver. Left England in December 1945 for New York; Kilmer, NJ to Fort Knox, KY. Was discharged Dec. 24, 1945.

Attended the University of Tennessee for two years.

Retired from the restaurant and hotel industry. He resides in Miami, FL. He has five children.

RUSSELL W. JACOBSON, was born Oct. 29, 1923 in Becker County, MN. He enlisted in the Army in March 1943 and received basic training at Fort McClellan, AL.

Was shipped overseas on the *Queen Mary* in July 1943; docked in Scotland and joined the 5th at Tidworth Barracks, England. He was assigned to L Co. of the 10th, trained in Northern Ireland until July 1944 when the division landed at Omaha Beach and began the Normandy Campaign, Northern France and Rhineland Compaign.

The Mosselle River Crossing at Arnaville and the Battle for Metz were the most memorable.

He was wounded Nov. 17, 1944 and hospitalized in England until April 1945. Upon release he was assigned to SHAEF as message center chief.

He served at Paris, Frankfurt on the Main, and Berlin with rank of Tec. 4. Jacobson was discharged at Camp McCoy, WI in November 1945.

He married Shirley Pernula in July 1946. They have three children: one son, two daughters and seven grandchildren. He retired from a banking career of 46 years in April 1992. He enjoys gardening, hunting and golf.

DONALD E. JEFFERS, was inducted at Fort Harrison, IN. He received infantry replacement training at Camp Blanding, FL. Training was cut short (12 weeks) because of the need for replacements in Europe. He joined K Co., 11th Regt. in Luxembourg and was assigned to the machine gun section where he served until discharged.

Was wounded in the Ruhr Pocket battle and evacuated to a hospital near Paris, France. He rejoined the division in the occupation area in South Germany and returned to Camp Campbell, KY with them.

Jeffers was discharged in December 1945 and awarded the Combat Infantry Badge, Purple Heart, Bronze Star, ETO with three Campaign Stars, Good Conduct Medal, and German Occupation Medal.

He worked 18 years as an operating engineer and 19 years as a supervisor in a rolling mill. He retired in 1984 at age 61.

JOHN R. JOLLEY, was born in Bowling Green, Wood County, OH and served with Co. M, 10th Inf. Regt., 5th Div. He participated in battles at Normandy, Northern France, Ardennes, Rhineland, and Central Europe. All of the above battles and his training in Ireland were memorable experiences.

Jolley was discharged on Oct. 6, 1945 with rank of staff sergeant. He was awarded the EAME Theater Ribbon with five Bronze Stars, Bronze Star Medal, and Good Conduct Ribbon.

Married 48 years and has one son, two daughters. He worked for the *Toledo Blade* newspaper for 36 years.

HERMAN JOST, was born April 6, 1907 in East St. Louis, IL where he attended high school. He went to three CMTC camps and joined the National Guard while in high

school. He attended Illinois University and was appointed a second lieutenant in the ORC. After graduation he went with a public utility company in St. Louis and was deferred from military service. However, this deferment was lifted when WWII developed and he was called into service on July 6, 1942.

Was given a one-month refresher course at Fort Sill. After this he was sent to Iceland to be a battery commander in the 50th FA BN. Then came tours in England and Ireland before going into combat in France in October 1944. He participated in Normandy, Northern France, Rhineland, Ardennes, Alsace and Northern Europe Campaigns.

Capt. Tom Cooper and Jost, along with two EM, captured 60 prisoners during the battle for Metz. Was wounded in the Frankfurt fighting and awarded three Bronze Star Medals, two for valor.

After the war he went in the 102nd Inf. Div. and retired as G-3 with 30 years of service.

JOHN KAMPA, was born on a farm in Barnesville, MN in February 1922. He was drafted in the U.S. Army on Nov. 10, 1942 at Fort Snelling, MN and took basic training at Camp Polk, LA with the 7th Armd. Div.

He was in the hospital in New York when the 7th Armd. went overseas. After getting out of the hospital was sent overseas as a replacement in England. After one month he was shipped to France. He landed in Utah Beach on June 27, 1944. After two weeks of infantry training he was transferred to Co. F, 2nd Regt., 5th Inf. Div..

He fought in battles in Northern France, Ardennes, Rhineland, and Central Europe as a squad leader. They lost a lot of buddies in the Battle of the Bulge and Diekirch. There were six of them left in his platoon when they were relieved in late afternoon in Diekirch after fighting around Kippenhof in late January 1945. They had to find the rest of their Company in Diekirch, most of the men were killed or wounded.

He served one year, one month, and three days in foreign service; and one year, 10 months, and 28 days in the States. Was discharged as staff sergeant on Nov. 10, 1945 from Camp Atterbury, IN. He received the Good Conduct Medal, Bronze Star Medal, American Campaign Medal, EAME Theater Ribbon with four Bronze Stars, WWII Victory Medal, Army Occupational Medal with Germany Clasp, Combat Infantry Badge, Expert Badge with Submachine Gun Bar and the Honorable Service Lapel Button for WWII.

He married Lucille Wunderlich on June 11, 1946. They had six sons (two died at ages 25 and 30 years old in accidents) and nine grandchildren.

Kampa was employed as a truck driver for 26 years delivering for Montgomery Ward. He is now retired and enjoying gardening, fishing, and traveling.

JOSEPH KISH, entered the regular Army from Hammond, IN on Oct. 4, 1939. He was assigned to the re-activated 5th Inf, Div, Arty., HQ Btry., the only unit in which he served throughout his entire Army career.

In the early 40s he took part in all of the division artillery peace time maneuvers and before the draft was on recruiting duty for several months.

He moved with the division artillery from Fort Custer to Iceland and promoted to master sergeant as communications chief, HQ Btry. Div. Arty. He then proceeded with the artillery to England, Northern Ireland, and to Utah Beach.

Kish served in all of the division's five campaigns and was commissioned overseas from enlisted status. He returned to the States in July 1945 and separated from the military in September 1945 at Camp Campbell, KY.

For 25 years he worked for Gatx, manufacturers of freight cars, and for Sargent Lundy Engineers Power Plant Designers for 20 years as supervisor of office operations. He retired in 1987.

WILLIAM C KRAUSE, was born in Cleveland, OH on Nov. 18, 1924 and raised in Drayton Plains, MI. He entered the Army on March 18, 1943 and took his basic training at Fort Jackson, SC. After being sent overseas on Oct. 15, 1943, he was assigned to Co. E, 10th Inf. He was wounded in St. Lo, France on July 30, 1944.

When he returned to the States he spent 18 consecutive months in Nichols General Hospital, Louisville, KY and Ashford General Hospital, White Sulphur Springs, WV, formerly the famous Greenbrier Hotel, where he was discharged from the Army on Nov. 17, 1945.

Graduating from Detroit College of Applied Science, he worked in the field of drafting. After retiring in 1975, Bill moved to Port Charlotte, FL.

He and his wife have four children and five grandchildren. He has a life membership in the DAV.

EDWARD G. LEHMAN, was born in Paterson, NJ in 1919 and inducted in the U.S. Army in October 1941. He received basic training at Fort Bragg, NC; transferred and assigned to Service Battery, 50th FA BN in January 1942. He served with Service Battery in Iceland on to the Normandy landing, Utah Red Beach, July 10, 1944. Transferred to Btry. A, 50th FA BN as ammunition sergeant after the St. Lo breakthrough.

He saw action from Normandy to Pilsen, Czechoslovakia, especially in regards to the Sauer River Crossing into the Siegfried Line, where he received a Bronze Star. Lehman was discharged in September 1945.

An interesting memorable experience which he observed on the Autobahn to Frankfurt was a camouflaged propeller, less aircraft off the side of the road. On inspection it turned out to be an enemy jet fighter plane which was hurriedly secured by the arrival of MPs.

He married Emily Jane Tullius from Oklahoma City, OK in September 1950. They have two lovely daughters and four wonderful grandchildren.

After 32 years he retired from Merck and Company, Rahway, NJ, as a research biologist. He enjoys the usual traveling, gardening, sports, and reading.

HORACE F. LOCKWOOD, was born Sept. 6, 1923 in Pompton Lakes, NJ. He was drafted in the Army on Feb. 18, 1943 and took basic training at Camp Croft, SC. He was sent overseas on July 25, 1943; assigned to HQ Co., 2nd Bn. 10th Inf. in

Tidworth, England. He was promoted to battalion message center chief in March 1944. Later on he became communication sergeant.

He received the Combat Infantry Badge, Bronze Star and the EAME Theater Ribbon with five Bronze Stars.

He returned to the USA on July 9, 1945 with the 5th Div. They were stationed at Camp Campbell, KY. He was discharged from Seperation Center, Camp Atterbury, IN on Oct. 1, 1945 on point system with rank of staff sergeant.

He became a building contractor and retired in 1984. He resides in Wayne, NJ.

JOHN L. LYNCH, was born July 27, 1917 in Urbana, IL. He graduated from the University of Illinois ROTC in 1940. He served at Camp McCoy, Ft. Sheridan, Camp Custer, Fort Hamilton, Iceland, England, Ireland, France, Germany, and Rhine River with 19th FA, 50th FA, 46th FA, 2nd Bn., 10th Inf ASLN.

He remembers the 700 miles sweep across France in the lead jeep to Moselle River and Metz; the Saar, Bulge, Worms. He crossed 14 rivers in rubber boats with 2nd Bn., 10th Inf. His most memorable experiences were Angers, Montereau, Cote De Faye, Pournoy La Chetive and Metz, where 2nd Bn., 10th Inf. was decimated.

He traveled home through LeHarve, South Hampton, Hoboken, Camp Dix, Fort Sheridan, Fort Sam Houston, Fort Sill after V-J Day.

Lynch worked at General Electric Company in civilian life. He is retired and remembering how they have forgotten.

ROBERT MALINOWSKI, was born May 30, 1939 in Dunmore, PA. He entered the Army Jan. 11, 1962 and took basic training at Fort Jackson, SC; sent to Co. B, 1st Bn., 61st Inf., 5th Inf. Div., Ft. Carson, CO. During Swift Strike III, which was held in the state of South Carolina from June 15-July 15, 1963, the CO breaks radio silence to the general and tells him he has a medical emergency, that Malinowski had a heat stroke. The general tells him to mark the spot so the helicopter could land. The CO tells the XO to mark the spot with smoke. The wind changed direction and the helicopter could not land. They carried him about a block and put him in the company ambulance and took him to the nearest hospital 40 miles or more away. After five minutes in the first hospital, he was refused medical treatment because he was white. He was taken to a second hospital, admitted for heat stroke, heat exhaustion and stomach problems. The three people who saved his life were: Sgt. Hammond, in charge of the ambulance; PFC Hawkins, the driver; and Pvt. Burgmeyer, the medic.

Malinowski was discharged Dec. 9, 1963 at Ft. Carson, CO. At the present time he is back in the garage business in Dunmore, PA.

JOHN RAY MANNING, was born in June 1918 in Philadelphia, PA. Was employed as a tool designer for B-17s and P-47s. Inducted into the U.S. Army in June 1944. He took basics at Fort Wheeler, GA.

Landed in LeHarve, France in January 1945. Joined the 3rd Army, 5th Div., Co. A, at Echternach, Luxembourg on Jan. 10, 1945 during Battle of the Bulge. He became squad leader, serving in combat and the invasion of Germany, Rhine Crossing, Czechoslovakia, and occupation until July 1945.

Manning returned to Camp Campbell, KY as platoon tech sergeant. He was discharged in May 1946. His awards include the Combat Infantry Badge, and Bronze Star with Cluster.

He married Edna M. First in March 1944 and has two lovely daughters and two grandchildren. He was self-employed 35 years and now traveling in his leisure time. Other interests are gardening and photography.

CHARLES R. McGREGOR, was born in 1920 in Warren County, TN to Lula Castella and Charles McGregor. He entered military service in 1941 at Camp Croft, SC. He served with the 5th Div. at Fort Custer, MI; Iceland; England; and France as a BAR man.

McGregor, an infantryman for Co. G in the 11th Regt. of the 5th U.S. Army Div., was listed as missing on Oct. 4, 1944. He was declared dead by the Army one year later, but his remains were not recovered until Oct. 24, 1989.

The Warren County native gave his life during an assault on Ft. Driant near Metz, France as he was part of the second invasion force following the June 6, 1944 D-day invasion.

According to the sole survivor of the mission, Sgt. Hugh Sykes of Clarksville, now deceased, McGregor was one of 49 men who perished when their company came under small arms and artillery fire as they were conducting a secret mission behind enemy lines near Ft. Driant, which was then held by the Nazis.

Sykes, who was McGregor's commanding officer, communicated those events, which were unclassified, to McGregor's parents in correspondence sent on June 12th and 15th of 1945.

As par of Sykes' letter of June 15, it was revealed that not only had McGregor served his country well, but he had been instrumental in saving Sykes' life.

He received the Purple Heart, Bronze Star, and Combat Infantry Badge.

FREDERICK P. McINTYRE MD, was born Sept. 3, 1915 in Brandon, VT. He joined the Army on July 3, 1943 at Carlisle Barracks, PA.

November 1943 he served Med. Det., 2nd Bn., 2nd Inf. Regt., 5th Inf. Div.; September 1944, relief duty (temporary) 50th FA BN Med. Det. and 19th FA BN 5th Inf. Div. November 1944 Med. Det. 46th FA BN, 5th Inf. Div.

He received training at Medical Field Service School, Carlisle, PA and 664th Tank Destroyers, Fort Hood, TX. He participated in battles at Normandy, Northern France, Ardennes, Rhineland, and Central Europe.

His most memorable experience was when their medical detachment got ahead of their front battle line and was pinned down in a sand pit by enemy mortar and gunfire near Ejamps, France and they were guided out of the sand pit by a back way to safety by a young French boy.

He was discharged on Feb. 21, 1946 with rank of captain. Recalled for the Korean Conflict, September 1950-September 1952, major to lieutenant colonel.

McIntyre is a retired physician and his hobbies include: raising roses, family and grandchildren and he is a ardent circus fan, following circuses like a kid.

BENJAMIN J. MOCEK (BOHUSLAV), was born July 4, 1917 in Chicago, IL and was inducted into the Army on April 11, 1941. From Ft. Sheridan he joined Co. G, 10th Inf., at Fort Custer, MI. In October 1941 he was transferred to Co. A, 11th Inf. He stayed in Co. A throughout the war in Europe.

He was wounded on July 31, 1944 near St. Lo, France. He rejoined Co. A, 11th Inf., in November 1944. Saw action at Normandy, Northern France, Ardennes, Central Europe, and Rhineland.

Mocek received the Combat Infantry Badge, Purple Heart, and Bronze Star. He attained grade of staff sergeant and was transferred to Co. D, 411th Inf. in July 1945 for return to the U.S. on demobilization under the point system.

He was discharged from service on Sept. 4, 1945 and worked in the U.S. Post Office until retirement.

GEORGE M. MOORE, was born in 1919 and lived in Waynesville, OH when he enlisted at Ft. Thomas, KY on Aug. 15, 1940. He and his brother, Bill, enlisted together. They took basic there with G Co., 10th Inf. Regt. before going to Fort Custer, MI.

After transferring to Regiment HQ Co., they embarked for Iceland on Sept. 6, 1941. They left there after two years and went to England and Ireland. While working in the message center he was promoted to sergeant. After final training and fully equipped, they crossed the channel and into France at Utah Beach on July 9, 1944. He found himself in Czechoslovakia at war's end.

With approximately five years' service, with four years overseas, and 11 months' combat, he was discharged on July 6, 1945.

He married Marie Abrams on July 13, 1946. They have two sons and one grandchild. He retired from General Motors in 1981.

WILLIAM MOORE, was born in 1923 and lived in Waynesville, OH when he enlisted at Ft. Thomas, KY in August 1940. He was 16 years of age. He and his brother, George, enlisted together. They took basics there with G Co., 10th Inf. Regt. before going to Ft. Custer, MI.

After transferring to Regiment HQ Co., they embarked for Iceland on Sept. 6, 1941. After approximately two years there the division was off to England and Ireland where he was promoted to corporal while training in Intelligence and Reconnaissance (I&R). They landed in France on July 9, 1944 and were in Czechoslovakia at the end of the war.

After approximately five years of service, with four years overseas, and 11 months of combat, he was discharged on July 6, 1945.

The highlight of his Army career happened in England where he met his bride-to-be, Morfydd Richard, from Swansea, Wales. When she finally arrived in Ohio they were married on March 8, 1947. They have three sons and seven grandchildren.

Moore retired from General Motors after 30 years. His favorite times now are trips back to Europe. He is most thankful to God that he and brother, George, returned home safely together.

JACK MORRILL, was born April 10, 1914 in the Flint Hills of Southeast Kansas. He fed cattle on his uncle's ranch in Steam Boat Springs, CO en route to California in 1935. In the spring of 1941, after receiving his draft notice, he enlisted in the National Guard, and upon completion of basic training in Camp San Luis Obispo, CA, shipped out to Hawaii in the fall of 1942.

He returned to Fort Monmouth, NJ for OCS in January 1943 and was commissioned a second lieutenant on April 9, 1943. He joined the 5th Inf. Div. as wire operations officer for the 5th Signal Co. in Northern Ireland about Oct. 1, 1943. He landed on the Normandy Beachhead with the division in July 1944, and on Aug. 10, 1944 he

was awarded the Bronze Star for establishing wire communication across the Main River under fire at Angers, France.

After a brief period of occupation duty along the Danube River following the surrender of the German army, he sailed into New York on July 29, 1945. Following a 30-day leave, he returned to Camp Campbell, KY where he decided to leave the Army after Japan surrendered.

He was discharged on Oct. 1, 1945. In January 1946 he became a partner in a garage and service station. In August 1949 he was recalled to active duty. On Jan. 1, 1951 he was sent to Korea on the advance party of the 40th Inf. Div. to relieve the 5th Cav. Div.. After six months he was reassigned to the Japan Logistical Command where he served until April 1954. He was then assigned to the Army Electronic Proving Ground at Fort Huachuca, AZ. In April 1958 he was assigned to the Military Assistance Advisory Group in Denmark. Following MAAG duty he was ordered to Headquarters Continental Army Command at Fort Monroe, VA in April 1961.

While serving at US CONARC, he was awarded the Army Commendation Medal for developing the Command Maintenance Management Inspection System (CMMI). He retired from the Army as a lieutenant colonel on Jan. 1, 1965.

During his career he was awarded 15 medals, including two Bronze Service Stars, one Silver Service Star, the Republic of Korea Presidential Unit Citation Badge, and the Republic of the Philippines Presidential Unit Citation Badge.

Upon retirement he became a franchised jobber for Frigidaire Sales Corporation. In 1976 he sold the business and retired on a permanent basis.

FRANCIS E. MORRIS, was born on Sept. 2, 1912 in Red Granite, WI. He graduated from high school and a business institute.

He joined the Army on June 9, 1941 and was assigned to the 5th Inf. for all of his tour of duty. He served at Fort Walters, Fort Sheridan and Fort Custer.

His most memorable experience was seeing the U.S. flag flying on the dock in Boston Harbor on his return home. He was discharged on July 2, 1945 with rank of staff sergeant.

He married Doris Morris (deceased). They had three children and one grandchild.

He was a sales manager and retired on June 1, 1973. He resides in Wausau, WI.

PAUL I. MURPHY, was born on Oct. 24, 1921. He joined the U.S. Army on Jan. 10, 1940. He was assigned to Co. I, 2nd Inf., 5th Inf. Div.. He served at Ft. Brady, MI; Camp McCoy, WI; Ft. Custer, MI; Camp Wade, Iceland to Tidworth Garrison, England to Newery, Northern Ireland, to Normandy, France. He was wounded in action.

Murphy was discharged July 3, 1946 with rank of PFC. He received the Combat Infantry Badge, Purple Heart, Good Conduct Medal with Bar, World War II Victory Medal, European Theatre of Operations Ribbon with two Bronze Service Stars, American Defense Service Medal and the American Theatre Ribbon.

He has four sons: Paul, Joseph, Michael, Terrance and two daughters: Jane Marcus and Kitty Bajkowski. He resides in Clarendon Hills, IL.

Murphy belongs to the Society of the Fifth Division, Company I, 2nd Infantry Association.

ANTHONY J. OSAGE, was born in Leonardo, NJ and enlisted in the U.S. Army in 1942. He received basic training at Ft. Bragg, NC and was commissioned an artillery officer at Ft. Sill, OK.

He was sent to Birmingham, England as a replacement officer. In 1943 he joined the 5th Div., 50th FA BN in Northern Ireland. He left for France in 1944 and served eight months in combat as a forward observer and artillery commander.

Anthony participated in four campaigns: Normandy, Northern France, the Ardennes, and the Rhineland. He was promoted to first lieutenant. During combat in Echternach, Germany, he was wounded.

He was retired as a captain and returned to his work as an accountant in New York. Anthony and his wife, Muriel, whom he married in 1941, have four children and a grandchild. He has been retired since 1977 and lives in Connecticut.

EUGENE PAGE, was born Sept. 24, 1919 in Tennessee. He was inducted in the Army on Jan. 31, 1941. He served with Btry. A, 21st FA BN and received training at Fort Custer, MI.

Participated in battles at Normandy, Northern France, Rhineland, Central Europe, the Ardennes. His most memorable experiences were 16 months in Iceland, a year in Northern Ireland and the bombing at Verdun. Was discharged on Sept. 2, 1945 with 112 points and the rank of corporal.

Today he is a retired dairy farmer.

EARL W. PATTON, was born in Alexandria, MN and later moved to Michigan. In February 1941 he entered the Army and took his basic training at Fort Custer, MI. He was assigned to Co. E, 11th Inf. In 1941 he accompanied the 5th Div. on maneuvers in Louisiana. Earl joined the HQ Co. 2nd Bn., 2nd Inf. in January 1942. He left for overseas, arriving in Iceland in April 1942.

In August 1943 he arrived at Tidworth Barracks and later was stationed in Northern Ireland. In July the 5th Div. landed on French soil. He was in the Battle of Normandy, Northern France, Ardennes, Rhineland, and Central Europe. He was wounded, sent back to a hospital in England and returned to Tidworth Barracks where he was assigned to the 98th Replacement Bn., 2902 Replacement Co. HQ, U.K. Base.

With 138 points, he was discharged in November 1945 with rank of tech sergeant. He was awarded the Purple Heart with one Oak Leaf Cluster and the Bronze Star.

He returned back to Vickers, Inc. of Detroit. From 1962 to 1972 he had his own business. In 1972 he worked for a school district in Michigan as chief stationary engineer, retiring in 1982.

He moved to Plano, TX and went back to the same work in their school district. He retired a second time in 1991.

LAWRENCE G. PECK, was born Aug. 24, 1924 and raised in Red Granite, WI. He was inducted on April 14, 1943 at Fort Sheridan, IL and departed for Wales in October 1943. Participated in action at Normandy, Northern France, Ardennes, Rhineland, and Central Europe.

He returned to the USA in July 1945

and was discharged on Oct. 10, 1945 at Camp Campbell, KY. He received the Good Conduct Medal; So. 6 HQ, 46th Field Artillery Bn., May 30, 1945; European-African-Middle Eastern Service Medal with five Bronze Stars.

After service he returned to Janesville, WI where he married and settled down, working for the Chicago-Milwaukee-St. Paul Railroad. He retired after 32 years in 1981 as yardmaster. His love for fishing and hunting lasted until he passed away on Feb. 14, 1993.

VICTOR PIGOGA, entered military service in September 1939 and was assigned to the 26th Inf. He went overseas with the 5th Div HQ to Iceland and was then transferred to L Co. of the 10th Inf. where he served until being severely wounded on Sept. 12, 1944. After three major chest operations he was discharged on Dec. 12, 1945.

After graduation from college with a degree in business administration, he went to work as a controller with a large bakery chain. Then, after 12 years he went to work with the U.S. Postal Service, retiring in 1983 due to his war injuries.

His lovely wife, Hattie, is an associate member of the Society of the 5th Division. They have a daughter, Carol, and a son, Victor, and three grandchildren.

SGT. JOSEPH PIETROFORTE, entered service from Philadelphia, PA in 1941. He took basic training at Camp Wheeler, GA and additional basic training at other camps.

He was sent overseas as replacement for Rifle Platoon of the 1st Inf. Div. He saw action at Aachen, Germany. During action at Battle of the Bulge, he was separated from

his company and was reassigned to G Co., 11th Inf., 5th Div. as bazookaman until the end of the war in Austria.

He was awarded the Silver Star for action at Erdof, Germany. Also the Bronze Star and Combat Infantry Badge.

In 1986 was reunited at reunion of 5th Div. in Tucson, AZ. He is historian for G Co., 11th Inf. He is still employed over 40 years as general manager of DeAnza Land and Leisure Corp., Los Angeles, CA, overseeing theatre, swap meet and shopping center operations.

JULIUS RAMEY, was born in 1924 in Elkhorn City, KY to Basil J. and Florence Adkins Ramey. He enlisted in October 1940 at age 16 and a half. He received basic training at Ft. Thomas with Co. F, 10th Inf.

He transferred to Co. I, 10th Inf., at Ft. Custer, MI. He served in Iceland from September 1941 to August 1943; in Ireland to July 1944. He landed in France on July 9, 1944. Was promoted to staff sergeant shortly thereafter.

Major battles were: St. Lo, Hill 183, and Moselle River Crossing. He suffered artillery concussion on Sept. 14th and spent one night in battalion aid station. He returned to his unit on September 15th and was captured on September 16th when forward position was overrun by enemy counter attack near Arnaville, France.

He was liberated from Stalag III-C on Jan. 31, 1945 by Russian troops. He started homeward on March 28th from Odessa, Russia.

Was discharged on July 18, 1945 and married Jerusha Hunt on July 26, 1945. They have two daughters, one son, and three grandchildren.

He had his own electronics service business for 25 years and retired in May 1992 from the City of Akron.

JAMES M. REISTAD, was born Feb. 16, 1920. He enlisted on Oct. 15, 1940 and was stationed at Fort Brady, MI with Co. K, 2nd Inf. Was transferred to Co. K, 10th Inf. in August 1941. Went to Iceland in September 1941 and stayed there until August 1943. Served in England at Tidworth Barracks a short time, then Ireland. He was hospitalized for surgery and transferred to Signal Security Section, Headquarters Advance Section Communication Zone.

He followed the 5th Div. across France. The capturing and entering Fort Driant at Metz, France was a memorable experience. Another was the "big" wind storm in Iceland.

Reistad was discharged on July 9, 1945 with rank of corporal. He received the Bronze Star, American Theater Medal, European Theater with five Stars, and Good Conduct Medal.

He retired after 27 years with Sun Oil Company. After more than 50 years the 10th Inf. still maintains a close relationship with an annual reunion and a "mini" reunion at Ft. Leonard Wood, MO, home of the 10th Inf. today.

Courage and fidelity.

DALE B. REX, was with Co. G, 11th Inf. During a skirmish in September 1944, Rex manned a machine gun for some 60 hours after being in combat for just 13 days. He also waded into the Moselle River and helped rescue troops while under enemy fire. Witnesses at the scene report Rex manned the machine gun post and killed more than 300 German troops, many advancing with fixed bayonets on U.S. servicemen.

When the order to abandon the bridgehead came through, Rex swam across the Moselle River. When he reached the west bank and looked back, he saw many U.S. soldiers in foxholes wounded or unable to swim that distance.

War correspondent, John M. Carlyle, reported: "So this Utah private, with the shells falling around, just stripped off his clothes and got into a boat."

Rex paddled in the darkness and saw a second boat floating by empty. He dove into the river and pulled it to his boat and towed it across. Some of the men cheered. Soldiers who couldn't swim put the wounded in first. Rex made four trips that night."

For his heroic action Rex was promoted to sergeant and then awarded the Distinguished Service Cross. He was also honored by the French, receiving the Croix de Guerre.

Rex, a native of Randolph, graduated from BYU in 1943 and played basketball as a 6'7" center for the Cougars. He earned honorable mention All-America honors in 1943.

Rex was killed in action Dec. 18, 1944.

DAVID T. REYNOLDS (BABY), was born in 1926 in Crestwood, NY. He was drafted in August 1944 and took basic at Camp Croft, SC.

He was a BARman, at age 18, in Co. I, 2nd Inf. Regt. He was in three campaigns: Ardennes, Central Europe, and Rhineland (33 points, seven months).

Returning from overseas duty, he became company mail clerk T/5 at Camp Campbell, KY and was discharged July 4, 1946.

He received the American Campaign Medal, EAME Campaign Medal, World War II Victory Medal, and the Company Bronze Star.

Dave married Jane Stukey in January 1949. They have two sons, one daughter and seven grandchildren.

He was employed by New York Telephone and later by AT&T (Westchester County). He retired 30 years later and moved from Valhalla, NY to an 1833 home in Hyde Park, NY that he almost has completely restored.

Leisure time is spent enjoying the family, singing with SPEBSQSA, restoring antiques, gardening, being "Mr. Fix It" for an antique shop and repairing old clocks.

RAYMOND L. ROYSTON, was born in 1912 in Hume, VA. He was inducted into the U.S. Army on May 27, 1943. Took 17 weeks basic training at Camp Wheeler, GA in the Infantry. He had five days' delay en route after basic, and went to Northern Ireland. On July 9, 1944 he arrived on Normandy Beachhead in Co. F, 2nd Inf. as PFC.

He married in 1938 and when inducted had a seven-week old baby son.

Royston received an honorable discharge from Camp Campbell, KY on Oct. 1, 1945. He received five Battle Stars: Normandy, Northern France, Rhineland, Ardennes, and Central Europe.

He retired as a maintenance painter at age 66. He has two children and four grandchildren. Since retirement he enjoys AARP senior groups and church activities. They have lived in Alex, VA for 47 years.

ROBERT C. RUSSELL, COLONEL AUS RET, was born March 27, 1919 in Akron, OH. He graduated from the University of Akron BSBA, and commissioned second lieutenant June 10, 1941.

He entered active duty July 6, 1941 at Fort Custer with the 5th Div., Co. L, 2nd Inf. Attached to 3rd Bn. HQ, Louisiana Maneuvers in 1941. Sailed to Iceland April 9, 1942, Camp Wade, Iceland Reserve, Force Tactical School. S-2 3rd Bn., Assistant S-3, 2nd Inf.

Transferred to 1st Bn., S-3 Operations; England, Northern Ireland Aug. 10, 1943. Landed on Normandy (D+30). Attacked Vidouville July 26, 1944. Assigned Patton's 3rd Army, 1st Bn. and moved to Nantes protecting 3rd Army flank turning east. Attacked Ammanvillers (N.W. Metz) Sept. 12, 1944. On Nov. 9, 1944 they surrounded Metz, into Siegfried Line Saurlautern, Germany. Luxembourg Dec. 15, 1944, Battle of the Bulge. Second in command of battalion.

Continued attack east crossing Rhine River where he was wounded and captured for 36 hours. Escaped to battalion and continued attack to Volary, Czechoslovakia. Cease fire occurred. Sent to contact Russians.

Was discharged on Oct. 2, 1945 to Army Reserve, with rank of major. He was awarded the Bronze Star, Valor with Oak Leaf Cluster, and Purple Heart.

Col. Russell, U.S. Army Reserve, chief of staff of 83rd Army Reserve Command, Ft. Hayes, Columbus, OH, January 1968-July 1971 and staff administrative assistant to commanding general as a civilian. Second in command June 1947 to June 1950 and Commanding Officer, 3rd Bn., 331st Inf., 33rd Div., June 1950 to September 1957, Akron, OH. Director and instructor of command and General Staff College, 2077th U.S. Army reserve School, Cleveland, OH October 1957-January 1968.

STANLEY E. SAMULAK, was born March 4, 1949 in Jackson, MI. They moved to Stockbridge, MI in 1965 and he went to work at Walker Manufacturing in Jackson, MI on Aug. 21, 1967. He was drafted into the Army on March 25, 1969 and received basic training at Fort Knox, KY and advanced infantry training (AIT) at Fort Polk, LA.

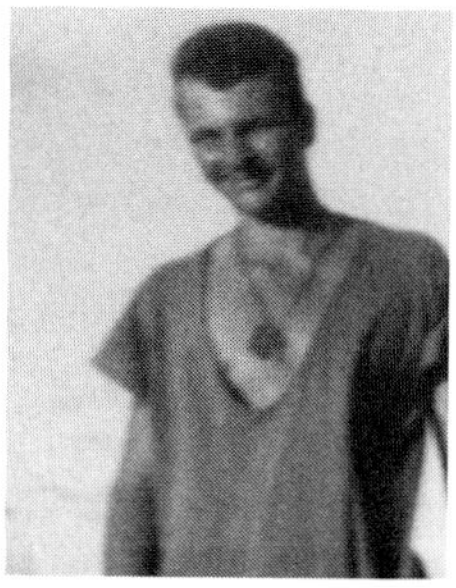

He was 20 years old when he arrived in Vietnam on Sept. 2, 1969. He was assigned to C Co., 61st Inf., 5th Div. (mechanized) and was in the Northernmost Province of Vietnam DMZ, Quang Tri. He was wounded Nov. 12, 1969 by RPG and laid in a field 18 hours before being rescued. They were outnumbered by at least three to one but made it out.

He received the Purple Heart, Combat Infantry Badge and Army Commendation Medal for Valor.

He spent two weeks on USS *Reppe,* hospital ship; one month in Japan 249th Army Hospital; and eight months at Valley Forge Army Hospital in Pennsylvania.

Samulak was medically discharged with 50% amputation on his right leg in 1970 with rank of specialist fourth class.

He is still employed at Walker Manufacturing. He is married and has a son and a daughter. He is very proud to have served his country and the 5th Div. Bloody Red Devils.

JOSEPH P. SAVENA, was born Sept. 26, 1924 and entered the service on Aug. 22, 1943. He spent four and a half years in action in France, and saw 14 months of action in Germany.

He was with the 11th Inf. Regt., 2nd Bn., Co. E, 3rd Army. He remembers that it was hell and has many bad memories of it.

HENRY SCHUSTEFF (HANK), was born in Hungary in 1919, volunteered in 1941 and was inducted April 3, 1941. He was sent to Fort Custer on April 5, 1941 and was assigned to E Co., 2nd Regt.

He shipped out to Iceland in February 1942, then shipped to England's Tidworth Barracks in August 1943. Was assigned to Cannon Company and promoted to gunner corporal before going to Ireland for additional training.

Landed in France July 7, 1944 and was in combat until after the Battle of the Bulge. He was awarded the Combat Infantry Badge and Bronze Star.

He was discharged at Fort Sheridan on June 12, 1945. He married Eleanor Halpern on St. Patrick's Day 1946. They have two children and four grandchildren.

He retired Jan. 1, 1991, after 45 years in advertising typography profession. He travels to all division and regimental reunions as time and finances will allow. He is past commander (three terms) of VFW Post 1612.

ANDREW SEMONCO, was born in the coal fields in Elkhorn, WV in 1923 and working at the time of his induction on Feb. 16, 1943. He entered the service at Fort Thomas, KY and had basic training at Fort McClellan, AL.

In September 1944 they were sent over as replacements in France and their company joined with the 5th Div. Many of them were assigned to Co. B, 2nd Inf.

His duty was to man a 30 caliber light machine gun with Robert Severt as his assistant. Two of their closest friends were

Kovach and Gordon who were riflemen and inseparable. Where you saw one you always saw the other. They were around Luxembourg in the Battle of the Bulge and were pinned down in a wooded area by 88s. Shelling was intense, branches from trees were falling and the smoke was heavy in the air. When everything cleared and they were moving out, he looked back for Kovach and Gordon. They were both dead. Semonco wishes he could remember their first names, but perhaps someone in their family will read this and know what happened at the end.

Moved on to Germany where his feet became frostbitten. Was sent back to the States where he remained hospitalized for three months. It was a long time before he walked. He is very proud to have been a part of the Red Devils.

Was discharged from Ashford General Hospital on June 12, 1945 with rank of PFC. He is married, has four children and nine grandchildren.

HERMAN SIMON, was born Sept. 10, 1915 in Louisville, KY. He was inducted in June 1942 and received basic training at Camp Crowder, MO.

He served eight months with the 5th Div. in Iceland and was transferred out to form the 576th Sig. Service Co. He served three and a half years as radio operator, chief switchboard operator.

Their commanding officer made it mandatory for all non-coms to give close order drill. Their radio section chief, M/Sgt. Thomas, was a whiz at radio but knew nothing about giving close order drill. While drilling them one day, he had half of them going one way and half going the other way. Huffing and puffing, he chased them down and said, "Halt, halt." They kept on marching and finally he yelled, "I said halt. Can't you idiots understand English? A simple four-letter word spelled H-A-U-L-T!"

He was discharged on Dec. 6, 1945. Simon received the European-African-Middle Eastern Theatre Ribbon with four Bronze Service Stars, Asiatic-Pacific Theatre Ribbon, Good Conduct Medal, and World War II Victory Medal.

Was married, wife is deceased, and has one son. He is now retired.

EUGENE E. SLOCUM, was born April 20, 1921 in Tifton, GA and joined G Co., 121st Inf., 30th Div., Georgia National Guard in 1939. Mobilized Sept. 16, 1940, the unit went to Fort Jackson, SC to Infantry OCS, Fort Benning, GA in October 1942 as a staff sergeant, class 160. Assigned to F Co., 424th Inf., 106th Div., Fort Jackson, SC in February 1943 as company executive officer. Was sent to France in August 1944 as a replacement.

Assigned to L Co., 2nd Inf., as platoon leader. He was wounded the first time on Oct. 10, 1944. Was company commander of L Co. on Dec. 24, 1944 when wounded by machine gun fire between Consdorf and Berdorf, Luxembourg during Battle of the Bulge.

Due to injuries, he retired Dec. 28, 1946 at Oliver General Hospital in Augusta, GA. He was awarded the Purple Heart with one Oak Leaf Cluster, Bronze Star, American Defense Medal, American Campaign Medal, European-African-Middle Eastern Campaign Medal with three Service Stars, World War II Victory Medal, Combat Infantryman Badge.

After returning home he owned and operated Gene's Galleries of Fine Furniture until 1979. Since 1979 he has played golf and traveled.

Capt. Eugene E. Slocum resides at 1705 Williams Street, Valdosta, GA 31601.

JAMES L. SMITH, was born Sept. 11, 1918 in Iuka, IL. He was inducted into the Army on April 4, 1941 at Chicago. Was sent to Fort Custer, E Co., 2nd Regt., 5th Div. Transferred to Med. Det., 2nd Regt. In the summer of 1941 he participated in maneuvers in Tennessee and Louisiana.

Embarked for Iceland Feb. 4, 1942. Stationed at Camp Lumley. Was promoted to staff sergeant and assigned to Winter Warfare the winter of 1942 and 1943 at Mount Eyjafjallajokull. From Iceland he was shipped to Tidworth, England; Rostrevor, Ireland; Utah, France. At war's end, he was in Volary, Czechoslovakia. He evacuated wounded to the 3rd Bn. Aid Station.

Smith mustered out at Fort Sheridan as a corporal on July 2, 1945 on the point system. He received the Silver Star Medal and the Bronze Star Medal. He participated in all five of the regiment campaigns, receiving a Silver Battle Star for his ETO Ribbon.

He married Germina Smith on July 26, 1945. They have three sons: Roy, Thomas and Michael and six grandchildren.

They lived in Charleston, IL where he worked for USI Chemical Corp. in Tuscola, IL. He retired in 1981 and moved to Rock Valley, IA.

ROBERT A. STOWE, was born in Belmont, NC in 1919 and inducted into the Army in September 1941. Went to basic training at Camp Wheeler in Macon, GA and assigned to Co. C, 11th Inf., 5th Div. at Fort Custer, MI in 1942.

Went with the 5th Div. to Iceland and on to Northern Ireland in 1943 for training. They entered France on July 4, 1944, and he was wounded on Nov. 16, 1944 at Metz.

He was then assigned to the 8th Air Force and served there until returning to the U.S. for discharge in October 1945. His awards include the Combat Infantry Badge, Purple Heart, and Bronze Star.

Stowe graduated from North Carolina State University with a BS in textile chemistry and worked for several major textile firms. Has resided in Barnesville, GA for the last 36 years where he was employed by the William Carter Company in their research department.

WARREN N. SWINFORD, was born April 5, 1947 in Mattoon, IL; was drafted into the Army in June 1967; took basic training at Ft. Leonard Wood, and Armor AIT at Ft. Knox.

Warren and his three best friends, William (Bill) Ryan, Rodger Atkison, and Jim Taylor were chosen to be instructors for the

AIT class following theirs. The four buddies were then ordered to report to Ft. Carson, CO in March 1968. They were all assigned to A Troop, 4/12 Cav., 1st Brig., 5th Mech. The following four months, with the exception of a short stint on riot control duty in Washington, DC, were spent in intense field training exercises prior to shipping out to "Wunder Beach," Quang Tri, Vietnam.

Warren and Rodger were transferred to D Co., 1st Sqdn., 11th Armd. Cav. Regt. in December 1968. While Bill and Jim remained with the 5th Mech. Bill Ryan was killed March 1, 1969 when his tank was hit by an RPG. Bill's parents, Omar and Lucille Ryan, of Walnut Grove, IL, requested that Warren escort Bill's body home for burial. After performing this honorble duty, he returned to Vietnam and his job as an M48 tank driver with the 11th ACR. He was discharged as an SP5 in June 1969.

He married Nancy Blacklidge in November 1969. They now reside in Plainfield, IN and have a daughter, Amy, and a son, Chad.

Warren joined the Indiana National Guard in 1974 and will soon retire as a major with 22 years of service.

MARC S. TARTAGLIA, was born in Italy in 1921. His family migrated to America in 1927. As a registered enemy alien, when called to serve in Italian Army, he joined the U.S. Regular Army instead. Went to basic training at Camp Croft, SC; graduated from the Infantry School as second lieutenant in March 1943. Served as training officer at Camp Wheeler, GA. Shipped to ETO, joined 5th Div., 11th Inf., 2nd Bn., K Co. as a replacement.

He was awarded the Combat Infantry Badge, Purple Heart with two Oak Leaf Clusters. He was re-classified limited service and remained in ETO until January 1946. Promoted to first lieutenant upon discharge.

He started a silk screen and lettering company in 1947. He married Louise Riccardello and has six children and five grandchildren. He owned his company for 45 years, now retired, his sons operate the family business. Tartaglia winters in Florida and travels.

WILLIAM WAYNE THOMPSON, was born April 1, 1908 near Belvidere, NE. Was drafted and entered the Army on Sept. 3, 1943; took basic and motor repair course in the Corps of Engineers at Ft. Leonard Wood, MO. Sailed on the former luxury liner, *Aquitonia,* to England early March 1944 as a replacement. Was scheduled for D-day invasion but red-lined when he fell and fractured two ribs.

Transferred to infantry which began calling for replacements from other branches. In September he landed at Omaha Beach and moved from one Repple Depple to another until boarding a vintage WWI train made to carry 40 men or eight horses. Went to staging area where assigned to Co. I, 11th Regt., 5th Div. Went east toward Germany, fighting in several skirmishes and battles, including the liberation of Metz, France and nearby underground forts.

Crossed the Saar River into Saarlautern, Germany, engaged in house-to-house fighting. Suddenly ordered out and thought it was for a rest, but were trucked to Luxembourg to help stem the German advance on the south flank of the Bulge.

A few days before the Bulge ended, his platoon entered a clearing and were greeted by raking machine gun fire. He became a casualty and, to date, has been unable to locate any of the platoon's survivors, if any.

His Army days from then on were spent in hosptials until he was discharged Oct. 4, 1945. His awards include the Combat Infantry Badge and Bronze Star Medal.

He retired in 1977 after publishing a weekly newspaper at Bruning, NE.

GEORGE W. THRELKELD, was born Jan. 20, 1918 in Waverly, KY; graduated from University of Kentucky (1941) with BS in agriculture; commissioned second lieutenant in the infantary and ordered to active duty July 1941 with Co. I, 10th Inf. Regt., 5th Inf. Div. Trained selectees until ordered overseas, September 1941.

Arrived in Iceland, transferred to L Co., 10th Inf.; transferred to Service Company, 10th Inf. and designated S-4 3rd Bn., 10th Inf. Was removed to Tidworth Barracks, England (1943), then removed to County Downe, North Ireland.

Regiment underwent intensive training, alerted for movement to Normandy, sailed on July 9, 1944 and arrived off Utah Beach where unloading began next day. Relieved units of 1st Inf. Div., then assigned to the 3rd Army and its dash across Europe. On Feb. 15, 1945 near Bitburg, Germany, was relieved of his duties and ordered back to the States for 30 days of rest, recuperation, and return.

The war over, he was redistributed to Camp Butner, NC and ordered to Camp Walters, TX to train infantry troops for the Pacific Theater. In February 1946 was released from active duty and placed in the Active Reserves.

Graduated from Command and General Staff College, Ft. Leavenworth, KS, 1967. Retired from Active Reserves, 1969, placed in Retired Reserves and retired from the Army as a lieutenant colonel in 1978.

January 1958, received an MS degree in Soils from Michigan State University. Was employed by the Soil Conservation Service, Dept. of Agriculture, as a soil scientist, working in Kentucky, Michigan, Maryland and retired from the National Soil Survey Laboratory and Soil Conservation Service, USDA, Lincoln, NE with 34 years service.

Married Marjorie Cornett on Nov. 8, 1947 and has two sons. Retired in 1981 to Bradenton, FL where he enjoys photography, genealogy, walking, and traveling.

WILLIE H. TILLMAN, was born Jan. 31, 1920 and raised on a farm in Decaturville, TN. He finished high school in 1938, went to CCC Camp in 1941 and was inducted into the Army Jan. 14, 1942. He took basic training at Camp Wheeler, GA, then went to Fort Custer, MI to join Co. A, 11th Inf. and went to Iceland, England, and Ireland.

Transferred to Co. L, 11th Inf. and went to France in June 1944. He fought in the battles of Normandy, St. Lo, Angers, Argone Forrest and Metz. He was wounded near Metz and returned to England Hospital. He was then sent to the 415 Air Service Sqdn., 8th Air Force.

During his time served, he received the ETO Ribbon with four Battle Stars, Good Conduct Ribbon, Combat Infantry Badge and a Purple Heart. He returned to the States in October 1945 and was discharged on Oct. 31, 1945.

Tillman returned to the farm and worked as a farmer, a part-time truck driver and a part-time carpenter. He is now a semi-retired farmer.

JOSEPH A. TOBAKOS, was born in Chicago in 1916 and at age eight went with his parents to Czechoslovakia where he remained until 1935. From the day he arrived

in Europe, he always had a burning desire to return to the United States.

When he did return, the job situation was not the best. After working at various places, he signed up for the Civilian Conservation Corps and stayed for about two years. In 1940, after his stint in the CCC, he decided to join the Army.

His good friend, Joseph Kish, had been home on leave and told him of his Army experiences at Ft. Knox, so when he enlisted he requested to be assigned to his outfit, HQ Btry., 5th Div. Arty.. From then on, they were together until the end of the war.

From Ft. Knox he went to Ft. Custer, followed by maneuvers in various parts of the country. In 1942 it was Iceland, then Ireland, England and finally, France on July 7, 1944. They fought through to the Czechoslovakia border.

Tobakos was discharged on June 22, 1945 with 144 points and the rank of corporal. He received five Battle Stars.

In 1948 he joined the Navy and spent two and a half years in the Korean Conflict in the CBs. On his return the local CBs Unit was disbanded and he joined the Coast Guard. He reached the rank of CPO E7 and retired after 18 years with a total of 28 years of military service.

He is happily married and has a lovely daughter, Lyn, and son-in-law. He retired from AMOCO, Whiting, IN in 1977. He has done much traveling, both in our country and Europe. He enjoys golfing, bowling, gardening, and bridge.

THOMAS B. TUCKER, was born Dec. 24, 1923 and is a life long resident of Escondido, CA. Inducted into the Army in July 1943, took basic training as a combat engineer at Camp Abbot, OR. He was shipped to England in February 1944. Landed on Utah Beach on July 9, 1944 and fought in Normandy, Northern France, Ardennes, Rhineland and Central Europe campaigns. Assigned to Co. B, 7th Combat Engineer Bn., he was wounded Feb. 7, 1945 at the Saurer River Crossing. He was discharged as a corporal in October 1945.

He married Mary Frances Reese in January 1944. The Tuckers have two sons, four grandchildren and two great-grandchildren. Tucker is the founder and senior principal of Tucker, Sadler & Associates, a 32-person architectural firm located in San Diego, CA.

He hunts birds in Mexico, travels and visits the battlefields of WWI and WWII in Europe.

WILLIAM ULLOM JR., was born on a farm at Jackson's Mill, WV on Sept. 12, 1921. Enlisted in the Army in October 1939 and received basic training at Fort Knox, KY. He was assigned to HQ Btry., 2nd Bn., 19th Field Artillery and participated in Dusty Sabine River maneuvers in 1940. The 2nd Bn. became the 46th FA Bn.

He moved to Fort Custer in January 1941 and became battery supply sergeant. Arrived in Reykjavik, Iceland in September 1941. Finally, in August 1943 he arrived at Tidworth Barracks, England. Was issued new equipment and on to Northern Ireland for additional training.

Landed in France in July 1944 and participated in the battles of Normandy, Britany and Northern France. Was wounded by artillery fire in September 1944 and evacuated to General Hospital in England. Arrived at Camp Drum Receiving Hospital on Feb. 18, 1945, then on to General Hospital Center, Camp Pickett, VA. He was discharged July 4, 1945.

He married Sally Ann Boyd at Wheeling, WV and has two sons. He is now retired after 30 years in the motor freight industry.

THOMAS VARGAS, was born in Chicago, IL on May 31, 1948 and inducted in the Army Oct. 1, 1968.

Served with the 1/61 and 1/77 Armor in Vietnam from 1968 to 1969. Received training at Ft. Leonard Wood, Fort Polk, LA and Fort Hood, TX.

In Vietnam he fought in Dewey Canyon Operation, Khe Sanh and along the DMZ. His most memorable experience was being the only survivor of an ambush in Vietnam and receiving three Purple Hearts and a Bronze Star for Valor and the Combat Infantry Badge.

He was retired from the Army due to wounds received in Vietnam. As a disabled veteran, he achieved the rank of E5 and was discharged in May 1971.

Married to Barbara, they have two children, Thomas and Christina. He attended Loyola University. Vargas has been employed by Allstate Insurance as a claims analyst for the past 19 years. He is currently involved in many Vietnam Veterans Organizations. He will never forget his war experience.

DON R. WALIN, was born in 1919 in Armour, SD and graduated from South Dakota State College in June 1941 with a BS degree in mechanical engineering and an infantry ROTC commission.

Was called to one year active duty at Ft. Custer, MI and assigned to I Co., 2nd Inf., 5th Div. as a second lieutenant. I Co. and the 3rd Bn. were sent to Iceland in March 1942. While in Iceland he was sent to Communications School, promoted to first lieutenant and assigned as communications officer for the 3rd Bn., 2nd Inf. Served as commo officer for 3rd Bn. 2nd Inf. during training in England and Ireland, August 1943 to July 1944, and combat in Europe with 3rd Army, July 1944 to June 1945.

Was released from active duty in October 1945. Promoted to captain, Infantry Reserves in December 1946. Received honorable discharge in June 1952.

He married Ardis Pingel in September 1941. They have four children and eight grandchildren. He lives in San Diego and worked as an engineer in the aerospace industry (Convair, USN Electronics Lab, Gen. Dyn. Convair, and Rohr Industries) from 1946 to 1987. He is now enjoying retirement.

KURT W. WALKER, was born April 2, 1923 in Pforzheim, Germany. He was inducted into the Army May 11, 1943 at Camp Upton, NY. He served in Northern France, Ardennes, Rhineland and Central Europe campaigns.

Walker was wounded in the European Theater Oct. 13, 1944 and again on March 28, 1945. He was discharged Oct. 22, 1945 with rank of staff sergeant. His awards include the Bronze Star Medal, Purple Heart with one Oak Leaf Cluster, Good Conduct Medal and the European-African-Middle Eastern Service Medal.

He now resides in Hackensack, NJ.

CLYDE WALTON, was born Jan. 14, 1919 in Frenchburg, KY. He entered the Army on Oct. 16, 1940 at Ft. Thomas, KY. He served at Ft. Custer, MI; Iceland, England, Ireland, France, Luxembourg, Belgium, Czechoslovakia, and Austria. He saw action from July 14, 1944 to May 8, 1945 in AT Co., 10th Inf.

Memorable experiences: a six-hour pass in Luxembourg City; a 48-hour pass from Luxembourg to France; seeing his younger brother four times in Austria.

Was discharged Aug. 20, 1945. His awards include the Good Conduct Medal, European Medal, German Occupation Medal, Bronze Star and Silver Star.

He went to work at Frigidaire G.M., Oct. 15, 1945. He married and raised two sons, who both served in the U.S. Army, one 13 years and the other 15 years.

Walton retired Aug. 29, 1975 from General Motors, Marine City, OH. His wife passed away Oct. 5, 1987. Has been a Christian for 36 years in the Church of God. His health is good and he resides in Camden, OH.

WILJO W. WANHALA (BILL), was born in May 1925 in Duluth, MN. He was drafted in July 1943 and went to basic training at Camp Stewart, GA with the 655th, AAAMG Btry., 15th Abn. Was shipped to Camp Pickett, VA for infantry training in January 1944. In July 1944 was shipped out of Camp Shanks, NY for Firth of Clyde and then across the Channel to a Repo Depot.

He joined Co. B, 10th Inf. the latter part of August. Fought around Moselle River and Ft. Driant where he was captured on Oct. 7, 1944. He was a prisoner for seven months at Stalag XIIA, Limburg and IIB, Hammerstien, Germany. While a prisoner he walked almost 900 miles. He was liberated in May 1945, Schwerin, Germany.

Married Betty Baker in January 1947. They have one daughter, two sons, and seven grandchildren. He worked 12 years as a cat skinner in Iron Mines, Hibbing, MN. Retired from the Postal Service after 29 years as a carrier. He is now enjoying retirement.

WILSON D. WARREN, was born Dec. 18, 1919 in Berlin, MD and was inducted in service Jan. 15, 1942 at Fort Meade, MD. Received basic training at Camp Wheeler, GA; assigned to Co. D, 11th Inf. at Fort Custer; field maneuvers in Tennessee and departed for Iceland Nov. 17, 1942.

Moved to Tidworth Garrison, England in August 1943; to Northern Ireland in October 1943 for combat training and July 1944 boarded for voyage to France off coast of Normandy. He participated in battles at Normandy, Northern France, Rhineland, and Ardennes. His memorable experiences was the Counter Bulge Offensive in Luxembourg.

Furloughed home with rotation group April 5, 1945 for 45 days. The ETO conflict ended, so reported to Fort Meade, MD and was honorably discharged June 11, 1945 with rank of tech sergeant, platoon.

Has been married 47 years to Mary Ruth. They have three children and five grandchildren. He has been actively employed in a hardware and building supply corp for the past several years. Warren still resides in the town he was born in, Berlin, MD.

ROBERT F. WEHRKAMP, was born June 15, 1920 in Sioux Falls, SD. He was drafted into the Army in August 1942 and completed basic training at Camp Robinson, AR. Was shipped to Reykjavik, Iceland to join 5th Inf. Div. He was attached to the Med. Det. of the 10th Inf. and received five weeks of intensive medical training. Was shipped to England, then to New Castle, Ireland in October 1943. Landed in France on Utah Beach July 8, 1944.

Participated in many battles across France, the worst was crossing the Moselle River. He was wounded by shrapnel and rejoined the 10th Inf. just before the attack on Metz. Crossed the Rhine River in March 1945, then transferred back to 217 General Hospital in Paris. Sent to Marseille, France and returned to the USA. Was discharged as sergeant T/3 at Camp McCoy, WI in November 1945.

Married and has two sons, two daughters and nine grandchildren. Was employed as employment manager for John Morrell & Co. for 37 years. He is now retired and enjoying golfing, fishing, hunting, woodworking and reading.

ROY D. WILKERSON, enlisted at Ft. Benjamin Harrison, IN Sept. 11, 1939 and assigned to HQ Btry., 1st Bn., 19th FA and took basic training with other battalion recruits. He performed various communications tasks. In January 1940 (after the famous Daily Bulletin Notice: "All men AWOL will return to their organization immediately"). They departed Ft. Knox, KY for Army maneuvers near Camp Polk, LA. He drove for an umpire and nearly collided with a sedan carrying General Marshall, Army Chief of Staff.

In June they returned to Ft. Knox and more maneuvers near Camp McCoy, WI. In September he drove Maj. Mitchell (Bn. CO) back to Ft. Knox. En route near Vincennes, IN, Col. Parker and staff were standing beside the road motioning them to speed up, but they couldn't because down the road two Indiana state troopers were pulling in between trucks and slowing them down until they were the correct distance apart! At Ft. Knox he became battery clerk, Service and Ammunition Battery.

Jan. 2, 1941 they left for Ft. Custer, MI. There the division had to provide a cadre for Recruit Reception Center, Camp Grant, Rockford, IL. So, lucky him, they departed on January 10th. He remembers watching Btry. A simonize the underneath side of their truck beds to help pass inspections at Ft. Benning, GA. In Louisiana they played "drop the handkerchief" with a garrison belt and you could hit the man who dropped it if you could catch him!

In June 1941 he married Violet Lawson, of Rockford. In November 1942 he was appointed WOJG and in 1944 went to France with the 1193rd Engineer Base Depot Group where he was in charge of a depot providing engineer supplies to the IXth Bomber Command and received credit for four campaigns.

He stayed in the service, was commissioned in 1951 and retired as captain in 1961. He then took a Federal Civil Service job and retired a GS-12 in 1983. He worked 43 years in all levels of supply-related functions after leaving the 19th FA.

GERALD A. WILLEY, was born in Reinersville, OH and was raised a farm boy.

Joined the ROTC at Ohio State University, 83rd Inf. Div. (USAR). Volunteered for service June 27 1951 and took basic training with Co. I, 11th Regt. Volunteered for Korea when sent to Japan in 1952, rank of corporal. Served with various units including 3rd Inf. Div. as a combat correspondent.

Willey was released from active duty March 25, 1953 at Fort Custer, MI. He received the Presidential Press Citation, EUSAK Citation for Meritorious Service, Commendation Medal, Good Conduct Medal, National Defense Medal, Korean Service Medal, Marksman's and Sharpshooter's Badges.

He graduated from OSU in 1954 and worked for Battelle Memorial Institute and Ohio State University Research Foundation as technical writer and editor.

He married Marilyn Lorraine Harris and divorced in 1976. He has one son, Stephen L. Willey. He is involved in volunteer activities and is a reader of the Bible and devotional books. He resides in Caldwell, OH.

COL. JOSEPH WILLIAMSON (MIKE), was born in Morocco, IN. A career Army officer, he reported as a lieutenant to 46th FA BN in July 1940 and transferred in September 1942. He advanced rapidly to rank of lieutenant colonel, commanding the 412th Armd. FA BN in ETO when WWII ended. He occupied staff and command positions in many countries until retirement in 1971.

Always active in military and civilian communities, he received many awards. Military decorations/medals include the Legion of Merit (twice), Bronze Star, Army Commendation, American Defense Service, American Campaign, EAME Campaign, World War II Victory Medal, Army of Occupation (Germany and Japan) and National Defense Service Medals. The National Council, Boy Scouts, presented him the Silver Beaver in 1964 for distinguished service to boyhood. In 1990 Purdue University presented him the Alumni Citizenship Award for strong commitment to community service.

He continues to be active in community affairs at local and state levels in Florida.

WILLIAM E. WILLINGHAM, was born Feb. 20, 1917 outside of Baltimore, MD. He was inducted into the Army Aug. 18, 1944 and took basic training at Camp Wheeler,GA. He was assigned to the 11th Inf., Co. G, 2nd Bn. as a replacement in Luxembourg on Jan. 28, 1944.

Battle actions included: Sauer River, Siegfried Line, Kyll River, Prum River, Moselle River, Rhine River, Frankfurt on the Main, Ruhr Valley Pocket and at end of war, Czechoslovakia Mountains, Occupation Area Southern Germany.

Willingham was discharged June 26, 1946. He received the Combat Infantry Badge, Good Conduct Medal, Occupation Medal, Bronze Star, American Theater Ribbon, Eastern-European-African Theater Ribbon and the World War II Victory Ribbon.

He returned to the States and Camp Campbell, KY. Attended Fort Benning, GA Infantry School for non-commissioned officers. Returned to his pre-war job and when the plant was closed, went to work as power engineer at a local community college. Transferred to maintenance department and became manager. He retired and turned his hobby of woodcraft into a small business. Willingham resides in Ellicott City, MD.

WARREN WOBECK, was born on a dairy farm in Greenleaf, WI in 1921. He enlisted in the Army in August 1940 and took basics at Fort Sheridan. Transferred to Service Battery, 50th FA BN in 1941 and was assigned a two and a half ton truck which was always a part of him from then until war's end.

In 1942 he was in Iceland and 1943-1944 in Ireland. Promoted to ammunition supply sergeant and landed in France July 7, 1944. Served 10 months of combat with 3rd Army and was discharged on 144 points June 18, 1945.

Married Violet Gohlke in September 1945 after 40 months V-mail correspondence. They have three lovely daughters, one son and five grandchildren who light up their life.

Was employed at Schlitz Brewery 36 years. He is now into 12 years of retirement and couldn't have asked for a better life. Leisure time is spent gardening, car servicing, traveling and reading.

WILLIAM S. YOCUM, was born March 11, 1917, a twin of Richard S. Yocum in Coal City, IN. He graduated from Indiana State University with a medical degree in 1934. Interned at Wishard Memorial Hospital in Indianapolis, IN, 1941-1942. Entered military service in September 1942. Went to Camp Pickett, VA (8th Med. Bn.) and served with the 63rd Div. at Camp Van Dorn, MS and Camp Blanding, FL.

In September 1943 he crossed to Liverpool, England with a medical officer pool. Joined the 5th Inf. Div. at Camp Jallalabad on Saulsberry Plains. Left there for Northern Ireland to prepare for the invasion of Europe. Trained at Castle Wellan, Northern Ireland with the 5th Med. Bn. Here he was in charge of building a road with rocks and the troops called it "Yocum Highway!"

He was sent to the 2nd Bn., 10th Inf. Regt. at Ballynahinch near Warren Point and prepared to invade Normandy. They left Ireland July 13, 1944 and went to Normandy to replace the 1st Div.

He was in five European campaigns: Normandy, Central Europe, Moselle, Bulge, and Seine River. He transferred to G10 Tank Division after the Moselle River Crossing for Pournoy Le Chetive, a very bloody and tough battle.

The war was over May 8, 1944 and he was sent to England to the 163rd General Hospital at South Mimns. He spent the rest of the time in ETO with Dr. Megenhardt.

Story of interest: 2nd Bn., 10th Regt. had crossed the Moselle River Sept. 12, 1944. They found refuge under a huge culvert. Milt Bartlett, Chaplain Sigers, and he were there with German tanks rolling around above them. Bob Brock, his Georgia cracker assistant, was present also. Chaplain Sigers prayed. They also laughed a lot, prayed a lot, and cursed a lot. Finally, they found a route up the hill and so ended their Moselle Crossing.

Discharged from the service in February 1945 with rank of major M.C. His medals include the Silver Star, Bronze Star, Purple Heart, five Campaign Stars per 5th Infantry Division.

Went to Lake County, IN and did general surgery, general practice there for 42 years (51 years as a physician). He delivered 5,000 babies and did 6,000 cases of general surgery.

Yocum and wife, Edna, have five children and six grandchildren.

JOSEPH J. ZANKO SR., was born April 29, 1924 in Perth Amboy, NJ of Polish parentage. At the age of 19 he was drafted and entered the Army on Sept. 10, 1943. After basic training at Camp Van Dorn, MS with the 63rd Inf. Div. as a medical aid man and rifleman, he was sent overseas as a replacement.

He arrived in England two days after D-day. After a short stay in England, he crossed the English Channel and landed on Omaha Beach the early part of July 1944 with a group of other infantry replacements. Zanko was assigned to Co. G, 10th Inf. Regt., 5th Div., 1st Army on July 14, 1944 as a combat medic and received his baptism of fire in the hedgerow fighting near the village of La Villeneuve.

At the St. Lo area, the 5th Div. became part of Patton's 3rd Army. During the fighting for the city of Metz, Zanko was promoted to T/3 and assigned to Co. E. On Decemer 19, Co. E was on German soil in the town of Wadgassen when they received orders to withdraw and hurry north to Luxembourg to the aid of the 4th Inf. Div. It was the start of the Battle of the Bulge. Despite the apparent confusion on dark roads, 80% of the troops were in the 4th Inf. Div. area within 24 hours of the issuance of the movement order. Their regiment's objective was to attack south of Echternach, passing through elements of the shattered 4th Inf. Div. When the war ended, the 5th Inf. Div. was in Czechoslovakia.

Zanko was discharged on Dec. 13, 1945 with rank of tech sergeant. He earned five Battle Stars, the Combat Medic Badge, Bronze Star, French Decoration and Medal of Verdun.

He still lives in Perth Amboy, NJ with his wife, Virginia. She was originally from Erie, PA. They have two sons, one daughter and three grandchildren. Zanko retired as a foreman in 1986 from the E.I. DuPont Research and Development Laboratory after 39 years of service.

He is a member of the Society of the 5th Infantry Division, the 10th U.S. Infantry Association, the Veterans of the Battle of the Bulge, New Jersey Chapter and VFW Post 663.

General G.S. Patton at the Rhine crossing, March 1945. (Courtesy of William Colon)

(Northernmost Publication Photo courtesy of Harry Scott)

C-43